RUN RACIST RUN

Dedicated to my dear siblings – Aiden, Geniva, Marilyn and Owen

RUN RACIST RUN

Journeys into the heart of racism

EUSEBIUS MCKAISER

BOOK**STORM**

ISBN: 978-1-928257-15-8
e-ISBN: 978-1-928257-16-5

First edition, first impression 2015

Published by Bookstorm (Pty) Ltd
PO Box 4532
Northcliff 2115
Johannesburg
South Africa
www.bookstorm.co.za

Distributed in the USA by Midpoint Trade
www.midpointtrade.com

Edited by Sharon Dell
Proofread by John Henderson
Cover photograph by Marius Roux
Cover design by mr design
Back cover author image by Mark Pettipher
Book design and typesetting by Triple M Design

CONTENTS

FOREWORD

At a recent panel on racism and the South African literary establishment, Eusebius prefaced his moderating task with reflections on the burden borne by public intellectual Black literati to constantly speak, moderate and chair panels such as the one he was introducing. For, whereas choosing a life of the mind means that we want to apply ourselves to the most pressing issues of our times, and oppression shows no signs of disappearing, writers also do more than think about oppression. They invent, fall in love, act badly, fall ill, discover, procrastinate and play. A long time ago, Njabulo Ndebele spoke about this as 'the ordinary' and argued strongly for its 'rediscovery', in what is probably the most routinely misread essay in South African letters.

A few weeks later, as we sat at the lunch Eusebius mentions in the opening pages of this, his third book, we talked longingly about the books we wanted to write, the ones we fantasized about and the compulsion to first finish other, more urgent tasks: mine, *Rape: A South African Nightmare* is now a few weeks old; Eusebius's *Run Racist Run* is the remarkable project you now hold in your hands. In an ideal world, they'd be out of our systems and we would now have the freedom to write creatively about more mundane human stuff. We laughed about the atrocious behaviour of a particular writer at an interview, talked about being in wonderful life partnerships in the slightly surprised manner that people like us (I mean creative, heady types, not just Black writer types) do, as well as about food, Catholicism, marriage, gym and allergies. This was the stuff of Ndebele's ordinary. It's also the kind of self-care Audre Lorde spoke about as crucial.

Of course we choose to write about the violence of racism, patriarchy, homophobia and nationalism. We decide to write about Black lives, being a woman and a man, being queer, and living in the country of our births. The last two sentences are not at all about the same thing. Read them again if you think I'm bluffing. I'm not. In South Africa, as elsewhere with similar enough histories, many of us speak of the enduring grip racism has on our lives as something we'd be thrilled to free ourselves from. This desire lies equally behind the rage, denial and defensiveness that otherwise seem at odds.

Perhaps, I am being overly generous about what many of us mean when we wish to be free of racism. Certainly, my own public and scholarly work shows how little patience I have for defensiveness that stems from privilege and silos. If I'm being kinder today, it is because even on second reading, *Run Racist Run* makes me hopeful. It is beautiful, brave and raw. It is also refined, risk-taking and funny. The funny bits aren't meant for everyone. And after you read about Black people, Judy Boucher and beetroot, you should finally understand what David

Dabydeen means when he insists that to write about Blackness is always more than a recital of victimization. If you still don't get it, read it again, even if it is only to understand that chapter is not about you. That's what Toni Morrison might say to caution against both the impulse to say 'it's not just Black people' and the assumption that your approval is required.

Readers of Eusebius's previous books will be familiar with how seriously he takes his writing craft and quality of argument. They will not be disappointed by *Run Racist Run*. New readers will be won by the risks taken by this Eusebius to show his own vulnerability, the invitation to take personal responsibility for individual racism as more than attitudinal, institutional and behavioural.

At the same time, many who are unwilling to walk their anti-racist commitment talk will turn away from the unapologetic prose in these pages. That prose partly stages a new intellectual romance with philosopher and Fanon scholar Lewis Gordon, whom Eusebius credits for some of the significant shifts in understanding racism. But it should be evident to more than the careful reader of this book that the shift is mostly evidence of the author's own commitment to rigour in philosophical reflection and really difficult, honest conversation.

On these pages, Eusebius McKaiser, philosopher, columnist, essayist, debating champion, and so much more takes on the big guns who've built careers on policing race-talk in the media. Racist personality is interrogated for its narcissism and its viciousness. There will be much anger, but the writer is unapologetic in what he demands from those who claim opposition to racism. And you can't fault the arguments he builds on their defence of white privilege whilst seeming to critique and reject it. You can see the distinction of a World Masters Debate Champion.

What you hold in your hand is a marriage of fine writing and exemplary intellectual work. I'm so grateful for this book even as I, too, wish Eusebius McKaiser's fine mind and generous heart had been free of the burden of writing about race.

Pumla Dineo Gqola
October 2015

INTRODUCTION: THE BURDEN OF WRITING ABOUT RACE

I wish this was not an anthology on racism.

I wish it was perhaps a meditation on questions about and experiences of illness, death and meaning. I wish it was perhaps my first attempt at fiction, telling the story of a Johannesburg man haunted by unconventional desire, rehearsing excellence in broad daylight, yet finding his most complete solace only in the comfort of shadowy characters away from the harshness of broad daylight. I wish you might instead be holding in your hand the results of a collaborative writing project with a philosopher-friend, aimed at helping us communicate more precisely, reason more soundly, debate more fruitfully, and speak more persuasively.

Racism, as well as discussion and writing about racism, drains me – emotionally and intellectually. So why can I not just wake up at five in the morning, anticipate the regular chirping of birds, listen to the energetic sounds of a waking Johannesburg, enjoy a cup of early-morning coffee, put on the writer's non-existent hat, and write philosophical essays about illness, death and meaning; or a novel exploring the choices we make when desire is policed; or a 'How to' guide for debating and public speaking?

In fact, I have somewhat prematurely been speaking publicly about my next book, provisionally entitled *Searching for Sello Duiker*. It is not just a celebration of the life and work of Duiker, but uses Duiker to tease out questions about illness, death and meaning. Some of you would have perhaps expected this book to be *that* book. So why did I write this anthology on racism?

I simply couldn't help myself. I felt a burning need to write a follow-up collection on racism, building on the essays in Section I of my first book, *A Bantu in my Bathroom*. This new collection raises questions I did not raise in that book and, perhaps more importantly, this book also represents a shift in my racial politics, and so it also contains many discussions on views I now think I was wrong about, as well as exploring views I had previously underappreciated or overvalued. I write about these shifts without any fear of accusations of vacillation, but comforted by the right – duty, even – to change one's mind as one encounters new experiences, sees the world differently, actively listens to others, and reads the work of those who have put in the same, or even a greater, amount of creative and intellectual energy, sifting through the subjects that also preoccupy one's own writing. Still, despite these perfectly good reasons, I hesitated. Because racism isn't a happy subject.

I remember sitting with my friend and intellectual crush, Pumla Gqola, at Nino's in Rosebank a few months before the writing of this book started. We don't see much of each other but we have a writer-friendship bond that cannot be killed off by our tardy attempts at seeing more of each other.

I was comforted by the fact that she too had potential writing projects gnawing away at her. It took some persuasion to get this charismatic professor to tell me about her current topics. She didn't anticipate coming to lunch to talk about her writing guilt, but I used my Catholic roots to get her to confess. In turn, I confessed too: that, although *Duiker* was coming along nicely, I really wanted to put it aside and immediately write a collection on racism. There was fire in my belly that I could not contain. But I felt almost compelled, not least because I have been advertising the *Duiker* project, to keep working on that instead. Pumla rightly persuaded me otherwise, and I set off from that lunch meeting with determination to write this book, and with more confidence in the view that writers ought not to ignore their inner voices.

After all, we do not make a living from writing in South Africa, and if you bought this book, you are a rare kind of South African, and I thank the non-existent man upstairs for your generosity. But I believe there is something happening in our country this year, the year 2015, that will in time be recognised as momentous, and this anthology, while not an attempt to cash in on news cycles (no good writing can come of that sort of cheap motivation), is certainly borne of the momentous events and conversations which I will describe shortly.

In addition to Pumla's advice, I was also encouraged by the reflections on writing that novelist Thando Mgqolozana shared with an interviewer early this year. When asked what he was working on, he described a collection of short stories, if memory serves. He was also co-writing a film script inspired by his earlier novel, *A Man Who is Not a Man*, which narrates the story of a man's botched traditional circumcision. Beyond that, Thando didn't know what he was going to write next, or write about, because he was very happy to write what he felt like writing when he woke up. Some of that writing might be discarded; while other writing projects would be completed. He seemed very comfortable to adopt, and live with, an attitude that affirms the voice inside him guiding his writing choices, and perhaps even dictating those choices. After all, those voices are ours; we only speak as if we have multiple personalities. So the advice, in effect, is to listen to yourself, to be yourself.

The same attitude informed Thando's response to some of the questions posed about the literary techniques he had played with in his novel, *Hear Me Alone*. This is a book, I am afraid, that I struggle to read, and will have to try again. But that is OK. Thando was very clear, and admirably so, that writers should beware the trap of thinking there is a winning formula that explains why a first book did well, either commercially or in terms of 'critical acclaim'. Thando's point wasn't that writers must be solipsists, or that it is desirable to deliberately ignore your past work or readers. Rather, he was warning against simply trying to reproduce earlier writing, and trying to figure out the 'formula' that resulted in sales. Readers should allow themselves to be challenged, and to journey with the writer as he or she does different things over the course of a writing career.

And so it is my reader-duty, if I take books seriously, and if I truly care for the work of Thando, to wrestle with the techniques he uses in *Hear Me Alone* that make it a tough read for some. It doesn't mean you or I must like the book, nor that the book will be immune to criticism, or immune to even downright dissing! But the general point here is surely correct: writers must not be anxious about past output as we set out to write, anew, every morning. This sentiment seems sensible to me and, combined with Pumla's irresistible energy, encouragement and cleverness, it enabled me to put *Duiker* aside and focus on this anthology.

In addition to these conversations, developments in 2015 presented another reason to hit the pause button on *Duiker*. Across South African campuses, we witnessed very active student resistance to the legacies of colonialism and apartheid. The #RhodesMustFall movement which started at the University of Cape Town and unsurprisingly moved elsewhere, will surely, in years to come, be recognised as a fundamental turning point in our national debate about, and in our self-examination of, the pace of transformation and elusive racial justice in our country. We cannot ignore the intellectual activism of students that we had written off as ahistorical and post-race. This sense of urgency on our university campuses demands a closer inspection of the non-bloody elements of racism, manifested in unchanged staff demographic patterns, curricula that have not responded to a post-apartheid educational agenda, statues, traditions and symbols that remain exclusionary, and other markers of colonialism's continued presence. This national context itself made it hard for me to 'take a break' from race questions and focus on, say, the meaning of life.

We simply *have to* talk racism.

RACISM THAT'S NOT EASY TO SPOT

Racism has never gone out of fashion in South Africa. While I find it hard, in the absence of trustworthy empirical evidence, to have a definitive view on whether the prevalence of racism in our country has been consistent over the years, it is inarguably still there. And there are times, like this year, and last, when a few very public acts of racism tempt us to think there is a definite increase.

You read news reports of black people being stopped in former whites-only suburbs simply on account of them being black and therefore somehow meriting suspicion for being in those neighbourhoods. Many residents have now even set up WhatsApp and Facebook groups to warn each other of the supposedly menacing presence of someone who is looking suspicious. Of course, this is just the familiar racist policing of black bodies. It is no different from the old white lady I wrote about in *A Bantu in my Bathroom* who rushed inside her house when she first saw me in our complex, before enquiring, nervously, from behind her security gate, where I was from. The message of her fear was clear: you, black boy, are dangerous because you are black. The same attitude is shamefully playing out in the United States of America where black men in particular are treated as dangerous objects by brutal police officers determined to wipe out black bodies. And yet, ironically, we're often told to look to the US to see where we might be in terms of race relations in about thirty or forty years' time. But the lesson about racism we actually get from America is that racism, despite key pieces of legislation declaring black people legally entitled to substantive equality, remains alive and well. There is no neat, linear progression towards racial justice anywhere in the world.

It is not just the policing of black bodies that has been reported on here. There have been physical assaults on black people too. One thinks, for example, of a white student pissing on the body of a black person from the balcony of a club; of black folks having to ask white friends to book tables for them at fancy restaurants which suddenly have space when white people call but could not accommodate black people moments earlier.

I don't know whether these kinds of reported incidents of racial hatred are proof of a spike in racism. One obvious possibility is that a few dramatic public acts of racism are highlighted more often in the media than before. My gut sense is that racism never declined. It just seems completely fanciful to imagine that centuries of state-sponsored and citizen-assisted racism could possibly come to an end merely because blacks are allowed to vote. Political rights do not guarantee less hatred in the hearts, minds, actions and attitudes of people. We have, I suspect, always been a thoroughly racist lot and we remain that.

What might have changed, however, are the ways in which racism manifests itself. And a central motivation behind this book is a desire to truly get under the racist's skin. Non-bloody forms of racism are harder to spot because they do not present themselves as visibly as a South African police member with a thick Afrikaans accent assaulting you with a rifle or setting those scary dogs on you. Apartheid racism was so visibly violent that we developed the wrong idea about what everyday racism looks like. I think many of us think, or believe unconsciously, that an act has to be overtly racist in order for it to count as racism. But that is utter nonsense.

And that represents one of the shifts away from *A Bantu in my Bathroom*. In that book I focused on overt racist actions and only in passing did I look at other manifestations of white supremacist attitudes. In this book I am much more expansive in my account of what racism and racist attitudes consist of.

The singular worst racist act, no doubt, is murder motivated by racism. But just like we had so-called petty apartheid – segregated neighbourhoods, parks, beaches, etc. – so too we have, if you will, petty racism to this day. 'Petty', unfortunately, is not a useful term. Because petty apartheid and petty racism are real and violent assaults on the dignity of the victims of racism. Petty racism, like petty apartheid, doesn't leave you with a black eye. But the inherent worth of the victim is attacked when he is asked, 'What are you doing walking in our suburb?! You don't belong here!' It is a serious act of racism even if no blood is spilled. In my experience, modern racism has simply become, for the most part, petty and non-physical. But it still cuts deep, and it is still pervasive. That is why I was tempted to call it 'non-violent racism' but rejected the term because all racism is violent. Perhaps the best we can do is distinguish between 'bloody racism' and 'non-bloody racism' or some such wording. But we miss huge volumes of racism if we think that physical violence is a necessary feature of racism, or that only the vilest words from racism's history, like *kaffir*, are the source of our problems.

So in this anthology I try to get into the nooks and crannies of racism. This is partly what makes the anthology, I suspect, a little harder to wrestle with than the six essays on race in *A Bantu in my Bathroom*. Although I already started focusing on attitudes and not just actions in that collection, I didn't drill down sufficiently into the unobservable realities of racism. In this collection I attempt to do so, which makes many of the claims I argue for in this book no doubt open to greater contestation. That is totally fine.

A SHIFT IN TONE, A SHIFT IN THE WRITER'S ROLE

I am angry. I am fucking angry. I am angry about the profound levels of social injustice in our country that refuse to go away because, between politicians, corporates and many wilfully ignorant citizens, we refuse to see the moral stains of the society we live in. We often pretend we do – a charity run here, fake integration projects there, and so on – but the structures of our society remain monumentally unjust. It's not that I didn't know this before. How could I only know this now? I see these injustices around me, and I come from the wrong side of the tracks, and I have close relatives living in tear-inducing poverty. What has changed for me is that I refuse, as a writer and an analyst, to treat any of these injustices as primarily intellectual challenges. They are not. They are real, material challenges and it is unhelpful, and frankly inhumane, to only examine inequality, poverty, racism, misogyny, violence and other ills *dispassionately*. A refusal to emote, and feel these injustices, is a moral and intellectual failure, in my view. I failed in that regard, many times, including in choosing a neutral tone for some essays in *A Bantu in my Bathroom*.

But because the smell of anger makes someone who is not angry think they have greater emotional and intellectual control over a conversation, I have made sure that this anthology includes an essay that specifically explains and defends the dialogical and moral value of being angry and expressing it. In that essay you will also find an exposition of why spaces for dialogue that aim at setting up a neutral tone are not always appropriate. I have, if you will, both emoted in this anthology, and calmly constructed an argument in defence of emotion. The critic cannot get away with complaining about being stung by the description of feeling. That would be a refusal to engage, and leave the analysis untouched, including the discussion on the importance of anger.

Don't get me wrong: there is plenty to be said for the instrumental value of remaining calm as you solve problems. Merely emoting won't help us to eliminate racism. I get that. And that is why I still want to be held accountable by the standards of sound argument that you find in analytic philosophy and competitive debate. I am not asking for a discount on the quality of my analysis, nor am I flagging my anger as an excuse for poor or unconvincing writing. Hold me to the highest standards of deliberation and writing craft.

But I do, in this collection, reveal more of myself psychologically than before, and I do not apologise for that. I suspect my normative convictions about the role of the writer have changed this past year. I am no activist, still, but I definitely feel, for the first time, a social duty to care much more, and more deliberately so, about the difference that writing can and should make if it is to be meaningful. My undergraduate self, which passionately protected the writer from attributions of social duty, is dead. I'd like to think of it as growing up, and letting go of the choking comfort of writing only with a view to constructing formally sound argument.

In philosophical terms this means that, while this collection contains intellectual argument, there is much more of an effort made, I hope, to describe the world as I experience it, and less anxiety about what we wish the world looked like. Besides, unless we have sufficient overlapping consensus about what the world we all live in *looks* like, we can't truly begin to think through the potential solutions for the most urgent social challenges we face as a society.

I rely once again on storytelling as a heuristic device. And I have included the stories of other people I have engaged and encountered, and not just stories from my own life. I have, for example, delighted in including a passage from a beautiful essay on the phenomenology of race written by a brilliant young black woman studying at Rhodes University.

When white people write complex essays we allow ourselves to put the work down, come back to it, discover new shades in their complex words we didn't spot the first time. This young woman's intellect deserves that kind of wrestling, and I simply refuse to translate her for you. Her brilliance is a form of intellectual activism against the racist.

SO WHAT DID I WRITE ABOUT?

The overall aim is to give the fullest possible exposition of the manifestations of racism in South Africa, especially non-bloody racism. Racism can be hard to detect in all its guises and we need to see the reach of racism in our institutions, in our interpersonal relations, in our attitudes and characters, and not only in overt public acts. That, in essence, is what this books aims to do.

One essay early on in the collection offers an account of the nature of racism. In it I distinguish between act-based accounts of racism and attitude-based accounts of racism. Without dismissing the importance of spotting racist actions, I defend a preference for accounts of racism that go under the skin, picking out racist attitudes, beliefs, dispositions and character traits. This essay puzzles through the true nature of the modern racist.

I think racism is so normal in our society that in one essay I offer argument for why it is acceptable to assume racism until we have evidence to the contrary. Lawyers, in particular, will find that thoroughly counter-intuitive but I think I provide reason for us to distinguish legal standards from norms that apply outside the courtroom. To refuse to accept that it is reasonable to sometimes assume racism is present in a typical South African scene is, in effect, to pretend that non-racism is the norm in our society.

A couple of essays focus specifically on white liberals. White liberals fascinate me because, unlike the outright racist who screams '*kaffir!*' with gay abandon, white liberals fancy themselves morally unproblematic allies of black people. But it is time to talk frankly about white liberals. One of the most coherent critiques of white liberals was Biko's and his views have been revisited frequently in public debate about #RhodesMustFall. Biko was deliberately misunderstood by a few people who thought he hated white people. His project was actually very sane. It was rooted in the need for black people to be genuinely autonomous, a project that requires us to be fully in control of our own projects, including the project of dismantling racism. Biko's emphasis was on the primary need for black psychological regeneration – *that* process couldn't be shared.

This means that white allies must play second fiddle to us in the fight against racism. We must put an end to having our hands held by paternalistic white liberals. Any white liberal who truly understood black consciousness got the point. A few didn't because they were not strangers to the arrogance more visible in outright bigots.

And that is why the white liberal appears prominently in this essay collection. White liberals remain a menace in the fight to dismantle the vestiges of our racist past. In one essay I skewer the pathetic demand of some white liberals that black people tell them what they can do to help undo the legacy of the past. This plea – to be given a formula for how to respond to their unearned privileges – is lazy and self-indulgent rather than evidence of self-awareness. A truly self-aware white liberal who wishes to chip away at their unearned privileges ought to think about why the plea, 'What do you want from me?' is misplaced.

In a separate essay, also engaging white liberalism, I ask more pointedly whether liberals are immune to racism. It's interesting that many white South Africans who helped to fight apartheid, and who hate undeniably racist people like Steve Hofmeyr, cannot imagine themselves capable of racism. That is why the foundational essay about the true nature of racism is important here. It guides us in picking out attitudes that are morally problematic among white liberals but which can go undetected if you only focus on overt, public acts of racism. White liberals often commit petty racism and don't notice when they do so because they think, in the words of South African writer Rebecca Davis, they are 'best whites' and best whites aren't capable of racism. I interrogate this lie.

White liberals are also so overly keen to demonstrate solidarity with black people that they sometimes, annoyingly, even appropriate our cultural memory, as I discuss in one essay. And then there is the failure to reflect on why whites disproportionately excel in business, and other aspects of South African life. This led to an essay that meditates on the myth of white excellence and meritocracy.

Among some of the remaining essays I also focus on the ways in which racism costs black people. In one essay, probably motivated, to be honest, by a need to counter my analytic white friends, I give an account of the nature and place of anger in dialogue, as I discussed earlier. I worry so much about whites that I even felt the need to explain black anger to the white reader. Go figure. But I also lament the impact of this anger on us. I deny Biko's mantra that we can write what we like as black thinkers; in fact, we are haunted by identity politics and not even fiction writers are spared. We also often mimic racists and bigots. Instead of remembering how hurtful it is to be discriminated against, we too are capable of monstrous behaviour, and the connections between racism and our xenophobia are also explored.

Until racism is eliminated, writing about racism will remain necessary. That means, despite my initial hesitation about writing this anthology, I have no regrets about having put *Duiker* on hold, as well as other fiction writing projects and a guide to debating. I cannot write what I like while the country is burning.

**(WHY) ARE BLACK WRITERS PREOCCUPIED
WITH RACE AND IDENTITY?**

**IS LITERARY APARTHEID A FEATURE OF LOCAL
RACISM?**

**DOES WHITE PRIVILEGE EXTEND TO THE
WORLD OF THE WRITER?**

BIKO LIED

I recently had a drink in Greenside, Johannesburg. A friend of mine, Amy, had my keys. I had forgotten these at a function we were at earlier in the day. When I picked up the keys, she asked me to stay for a drink. I obliged. She was with another friend of hers, someone I did not know. He was a white South African male, bisexual and dating a coloured woman. Amy is very charismatic and full of laughter, and she volunteered this information on his behalf within the first minutes of us meeting. I think it was an attempt to say, 'Guys, get on with being comfortable with each other immediately because you have, like, stuff in common!'

Except, Amy miscalculated. This dude – call him John – asked me what book project I was busy with. I told him that, actually, it was a long and complicated story. He seemed eager and so I told him I was busy writing a book on illness, death and the meaning of life. He seemed genuinely fascinated by those themes and wanted to know how on earth I had chosen these topics, and what I was hoping to say and achieve in the book. Because he seemed so interested in my work, I told him about my decision to put that book on ice. Instead, I announced, I was writing an anthology on racism, a collection of essays that built upon the first part of *A Bantu in my Bathroom.*

Having almost completed the entire book at that point in time, I was excited to talk to an interested person – like John – about it. I was ready to explain how the book had demanded to be written, and why the kinds of issues I raise and explore were distinct from any of the questions I had tackled before, or had been discussed in any public discourse on race. But the fucker dampened my enthusiasm before I had a chance.

He rolled his eyes. 'Racism! Aaaah. That's so boring! Surely racism isn't a thing anymore? No one cares about racism. Everyone cares about illness and death, though!'

I was raging mad. Not because, obviously, he would not help my book sales, but because he illustrated a brutal reality: that whites can afford to pretend that racism isn't a thing. Just like men can pretend that sexism isn't a thing, and just like homophobes can pretend that being gay 'isn't an issue anymore'; so, too, white people can afford to be wilfully ignorant about the reality of racism.

Not all whites were or are perpetrators of anti-black racism. However, all whites benefited, and still benefit, from the history of anti-black oppression. Two profoundly vicious consequences flow from this: many whites are blind to racism's continued presence; and, related to this blindness, many whites rationalise their ignorance by thinking that black people are 'race-obsessed'. Not only does John fail to examine how *our collective experience of racism's history* affected him, personally, but he has the audacity to be casually and confidently dismissive of the possibility that racism could be a significant, horrid truth for other people, every day.

As my late mom would have put it, I took him to the cleaners. 'Racism doesn't matter to YOU, because you're white and you can afford not to see racism or not even think about it. I don't have that luxury, OK? It's no different, buddy, from you and me dismissing women who write about sexism. Because we happen to be born with penises and the world is structured to advantage us and oppress women, we can roll our eyes at sexism. That's exactly the same with racism. If you think it isn't an issue any more, I suggest you take time to speak to black people instead of assuming you know our lives. Use it. Don't use it.'

I have zero regrets about making him go red. He asked for it. He deserved it. No, I am perhaps slightly too generous here. He didn't deserve me explaining to him what he ought to know. I did him a favour. I don't think black people have a duty to convince whites that racism is a reality. We need to get on with strategies for dismantling racism's legacy. White allies in the fight against racism are useful and important. But it is a bonus to have a black person explaining 'race' to you, or why and how you are wilfully ignorant about racism, and why racism matters. And I am not even sure John is an ally, let alone an ally with blind spots. So while I was mad at John, I actually did more than I needed to. I could, just as acceptably, simply have chuckled, not upset the convivial Greenside pub atmosphere, and said, 'John, let's drink bud! BARMAN!'

Amy was wrong in her unreflective assumption that John and I could get along because we were both not straight, and because he was in an interracial relationship. You don't have to be straight to be bigoted or ignorant. And being in an interracial relationship doesn't mean you grasp the ways in which racism continues to play out. And, for Amy, an additional lesson, perhaps, was that as an ally in the fight against racism, there is a greater level of vigilance required in spotting and rupturing non-bloody manifestations of racism among white friends than you might have realised.

The encounter with John has remained with me because I had all along felt ambivalent about writing this collection on racism, and his dismissiveness took me back to that place of doubt. I was, until I actually started working on it, excited about *Searching for Sello Duiker,* a book that was neither overtly about South African politics nor about race. It took enormous resolve not to care about people like John who would roll their eyes at another book on 'the race question'. (Not that people like John have necessarily read any other books on race.)

What the Johns of the world do not know is that black writers who have any self-awareness about the world in which they live and work cannot just let go of the race question. Because race continues to haunt us. And while it would be wonderful to write about a greater range of subjects – and, to be sure, many black writers can and do – there will never be a shortage of black writing on race and racism.

So, in a way, this essay is a meditation on the black writer's preoccupation with race. The legacy of racism is so darn powerful and ubiquitous that it extends as a matter of course to the world of the writer. Contrary to popular assumption, many of us do not wake up and freely choose what to write. Our writing is in part a reflection of the world we live in, coupled with unique biographical facts about each writer. I want to both describe and defend the apparent preoccupation of black writers with questions of identity in general, and with race in particular. It is, in complex ways, a preoccupation that flows from the history of anti-black racism itself, and that history's reach into present reality.

MY ENVY OF WHITE WRITERS

I am sometimes jealous of white writers. Take Rebecca Davis whose first book, *Best White and Other Anxious Delusions*, is a great exposition of folly, nonsense, and much sense, delivered in laughter-inducing sentences that inform and delight.

Davis writes about everything – from picking berries as a student on a gap year in England, to her hilarious regret that we do not have a universal way of greeting each other – one that transcends cultural, geographic and individual boundaries. There's always that awkward moment when you approach a stranger ready to give 'em a hug, only for them to stretch out their hand! I was unable to stop myself publicly laughing out loud when I read that gem about thirty seconds after I had concluded a business lunch at Primi in Rosebank, Johannesburg. The lunch was a great success, so much so that the woman I had met for the first time felt like a long-lost friend. And, when we parted, I was SO ready to give her a full hug. When I finally did, after playing out the anxious scenario in my head, it was lank awkward!

Davis dares to write funny but incisive *nonsense* in *Best White*. Like how fairy tales are absolute bullshit! Her discussion of the plot weaknesses and moral deficiencies of *Goldilocks and the Three Bears* is so delicious that I have now resorted to reading her work out loud to friends, complete with dramatic voice changes for the different characters, and every time, I cry *snot en trane* with pleasure.

Davis wonders aloud about how weird it is that three bowls of porridge dished up at basically the same time could possibly have 'reached vastly different resting temperatures minutes later?' After a paragraph of hilarity about the improbabilities here she asks for help from those of you who know a bit of science. 'What's going on here, scientists? This is horseshit, pure and simple.'

It's not that Davis is *literally* writing bullshit. Davis is funny, but her nuggets are also serious insights – into feminism, language, interpersonal interactions, online dating, television offerings, parenting, meeting the Queen, mansplaining (the misogynistic habit of us men of explaining everything to women as if they cannot be experts at anything, including their own careers, lives and bodies), tattoos, museums, the modern dislike of voicemail and phone conversations, Kindles and our new reading habits, dictionaries, and other day-to-day issues.

There are many writers like Davis who induce a kind of envy in me. Tom Eaton and Daryl Bristow-Bovey are two of the country's other excellent bullshit columnists. Eaton, the lucky bastard, even has a funny face to go with his bottomless pit of incisive humour.

Eaton writes about everything from childhood recollections of primary school to growing up in Cape Town. Like this:

> ' … some cities demand those kinds of tributes, essays full of fist fights with transvestite neo-Nazi dwarfs, written at 3 am in a cloud of throat-shredding home-rolled fags. Perhaps Cape Town deserves something like that. But it won't be getting it from me.
>
> It's not that I haven't fought with neo-Nazi dwarfs – I have, and my kindergarten teacher still remembers how the Cheney twins cried after I took the last set of angel wings out of the dress-up drawer.
>
> But it turns out that a life spent in a city can boil down to bouncing like a pinball between the same 15 or 20 addresses in the same five suburbs, having similar conversations with similar people. Those addresses are important to me, and those people dear, but do you care? I would hope not … '[1]

Eaton also writes about cricket, soccer, our obsessions with being led as people (' … like domesticated dogs we have had

---

1   http://www.timeslive.co.za/thetimes/2013/07/16/mother-of-a-city

dependence bred into us … '), diets, Table Mountain, nostalgia, and so forth.

Darrel Bristow-Bovey's output is a variation on the bullshit theme. He too writes a column, and books, that effortlessly move between reflections on midlife crises, letter-writing, love stories, Sea Point, the internet, inventing words, and so on.

Ah, to have the luxury of waking up in the morning and writing about the non-existing daffodils outside my window, a vignette on falling in love, an essay on good coffee, or what the most awesome sarmies were at school, filling Granddad's pipe with BB tobacco, watching *The Bold and the Beautiful* religiously, and other nonsense. But I don't. And I can't. I do not have the psychological and literary freedom of white writers to be carefree.

If you're white you can write what you like. If you're black, you can't write what you like. Steve Biko lied to us.

IDENTITY POLITICS, IDENTITY WRITINGS

It's not that no white writers write about race and identity politics. Nor that black writers cannot or do not ever write about bullshit. Last time I checked, Ndumiso Ngcobo was black. He writes about nonsense every week in the *Sunday Times*. Hilarious nonsense. Insightful nonsense. And he's not imitating white writers, stealing their formula to sell books, or to demand an increase in wages from the *Sunday Times*.

Ngcobo is *very* black. Have you seen my Zulu friend with

his imposing figure (well, the *mkhaba* is threatening to subside now, but still) – a physical presence as overwhelming as his raucous laughter, and a big heart he shows off on his sleeve just above his hand holding a beer that refuses to empty? He has the capacity to capture, like Davis, Eaton and Bristow-Bovey, the minutiae of daily life in bite-sized chunks that please and engage, before you return to the horrible bits in a newspaper about Bafana Bafana losing again, or the millionth earnest 'thought piece' predicting that the tripartite alliance is on the brink, *again*, of splitting like peas in a pod, *gatvol* of breathing down one another's necks.

But Ngcobo is an exception. Exceptions can be fascinating but obscure patterns. It is far more likely that black writing will be about identity and, in particular, our lived racial realities. Rehana Rossouw's debut novel *What Will People Say?* is unsurprisingly about coloured identity, as we observe the dramas of the Fourie family in Hanover Park in Cape Town in 1986. There are many aspects of this family's life that are not unique to the coloured community – like teenagers falling in love – but the full texture of this stunning novel can only be appreciated if a reader gets the coloured context within which otherwise universal themes are located. You cannot escape the particularities of the coloured experience in this novel. And this, of course, is not surprising. It is the apartheid racial legacy from which Rossouw's own life flows, and where her memories reside, and which have now found expression in this creative achievement.

Rossouw's is also a very funny book, despite the political

and socio-economic anxieties of the time and place. It is a novel written in the dialect of the Cape Flats, and the humour partly piggybacks on the familiarity of the characters. Sometimes we laugh not because what we read is humour as such but simply because we recognise ourselves and, for some inexplicable reason, human beings laugh when they see themselves on television, in books, or in the stories being talked about on radio. Recognition as a source of amusement.

Rossouw's novel deals with the horrors of gangs, children's education disrupted by political boycotts, drugs messing up life in our communities, love in a time of working-class struggles, the effects of apartheid geography on how coloured people view and interact with other races, and, more generally, her novel depicts the tropes of coloured life. It reminded me of my childhood and the continuing realities of coloured struggles that I try to forget about as an adult so I can also have some chance at writing, one day, about coffee or daffodils, and take a break from identity politics.

BUT ... Black writers cannot switch off their racial realities as easily as Eskom can switch off the lights. White writers do not have to worry about switching off their racial realities because, well, race doesn't haunt the white writer. Or, rather, whiteness doesn't produce the same effects in white writers. That is one of the unearned privileges of white writing.

My intention is not to lament works of fiction from black writers that depict and engage our lived realities. And there are many examples one could puzzle through in that regard: Kopano Matlwa's *Coconut* shows us the anxieties and tribulations of black youth, much of which they encounter when entering white urban spaces, be these suburbs or institutions, educational or corporate spaces, that were previously whites-only and which have retained institutional identities that are racially and culturally homogenous. *A Man Who is Not a Man* by Thando Mgqolozana is a powerful portrayal and interrogation of a traditional rite of passage gone awry. Not only do many young black boys undergo the ritual successfully, large numbers of these boys, tragically, also end up with botched circumcisions, and anyone who dares not go through with such a ritual can incur the social wrath of their community. A novel of this stature rehearses the politics of cultural identity. We could easily have added many other examples: Sello Duiker, Phaswane Mpe, Pumla Gqola, Niq Mhlongo, Siphiwo Mahala, Fred Khumalo, and many others.

And when I say 'typical of black writing' I certainly don't mean to impugn the preoccupation with identity. It is unsurprising, acceptable and even praiseworthy for writing to be located where we live. I think part of my puzzle with much white writing is that the luxury to write 'nonsense' is evidence of writers coming from divided geographies, from different South Africas.

APARTHEID GEOGRAPHY, LITERARY APARTHEID

South Africans live apart, obviously, and for obvious reasons: our history of racism manifests itself, in part, as apartheid geography. Apartheid geography has not been dismantled. It has its origins in the spatial planning of apartheid architects, town planners, and other administrative foot soldiers in the service of colonial and apartheid ideologies.

Racism's philosophical sponsors, like HF Verwoerd, thought there was a moral hierarchy among race groups and that it would defile whites – who are morally superior to the rest of us, supposedly – to live with and among us lesser mortals. And so apartheid geography was imagined, internalised by these racists as morally necessary, and executed by the racist foot soldiers in the state.

This legacy remains. Good luck spotting a white resident in Soweto. And if you do, they are probably only there for a six-month stint, blogging the experience in a comical attempt to seem like they are a better white person than their white peers who would not dare to set foot in Soweto. Of course, they mistake their voyeurism in Soweto for an exemplary and authentic experience of racial integration.

Equally, while you have a much higher chance of spotting black people in some of the gated communities of northern Johannesburg, the numerical majority of people in these gated communities is white, despite the fact that not more than ten per cent of the South African population is white. I have now lived in three different complexes in Sandton since arriving in

Johannesburg around 2008. In each one of these complexes at least ninety per cent of my fellow residents are white. The point is that no one should ever fool you, nor should you fool yourself, about significant integrated housing and integrated suburbs in South Africa. Apartheid geography is as real as it has ever been.

But physical space is not the only kind of space that is divided racially. We live apart in other ways too: linguistically, culturally, etc. We're pretty good at masking these divisions when we want to, of course, such as a racially mixed group of workers having a jolly time at a long table in a restaurant in Rosebank or Melrose Arch when it is time for the obligatory annual Christmas lunch. But these moments of conviviality don't change the fact that we drive home to different parts of the city. We go our separate ways as soon as the office party is over. And if you look carefully, you will see that many of these tables are caricatures of the city landscape: blacks bunched at the end, fed up with pretending they care for colleagues wearing that white smiley thing on their faces; white managers near the head of the table, pretending they are leaders of a company with values such as 'diversity' at the heart of organisational culture; and in between, a racially mixed few who went to former whites-only schools where black kids learned the grammar of whiteness they now show off at the end-of-year party.

Actually, we don't really know one another very well and we negotiate our divisions politely rather than make sincere attempts to live in the worlds of people who look very different

29

from ourselves. This same apartheid geography applies to literature and explains, in part, the different preoccupations of black and white writing I have discussed.

There is literary apartheid in South Africa that we do not speak about. It shouldn't surprise us that the worlds of writers are similar to the worlds of other South Africans. After all, why would writers be immune to the truths of the society about which they write, from which they draw, and in which they are located?

Davis, Eaton and Bristow-Bovey live in a different literary world from Matlwa, Rossouw and Mgqolozana. And that is because, in the physical world, they live apart too. And while these six writers might be more integrated in the physical world than many other South Africans, they cannot escape the history of apartheid geography just because they bump into one another at a literary festival, and maybe share a drink at a pub or interact on Facebook. (Mind you, even at literary festivals you will see black writers quickly finding one another to escape the unbearable whiteness of the local literary landscape. Don't believe me? Go stalk the minority black writers at most local festivals and you will see a microcosm of apartheid geography.)

THE FEAR OF 'RACE OBSESSION'

Sometimes we try as black writers to divest ourselves of the burdens that racism's history has saddled us with. If you take the legendary columns of Fred Khumalo, for example, they are often a laugh-a-minute. Many of them are about topics that seem frivolous and apolitical, like *Idols SA* judge and choreographer Somizi Mhlongo's appreciation of men in the steam room of a gym. Of course, many people can point to examples, especially in democratic South Africa, of black writers who do not portray black life solely and wholly *politically*.

Except, that is wishful thinking for the most part. Niq Mhlongo's novel, *After Tears,* may not be overtly about party politics or a comment on anti-black racism, but that is only because good fiction is never literal. You have to read with your eyes wide open and brain fully activated to see the various layers. This novel is an uncanny anticipation of the pressures that led to someone like former minister of Arts and Culture, Dr Pallo Jordan, turning out to be, in fact, *Mr* Jordan. And by pressures I do not mean to excuse Mr Jordan but simply to hint at the existence of a story accounting for how he came to live a lie around his academic qualifications. Still, Mr Jordan remains a self-confessed liar who behaved unethically even after being busted, attempting to bribe a journalist to make the revelation disappear before it could be published.

It's not that whites do not or cannot lie about their qualifications; many do. The point is that black frauds are spotted and skewered more quickly than white ones *because* apartheid has instilled in us an expectation that blacks are liars and frauds until proven otherwise. After all, we are not as morally virtuous, hey Verwoerd, as white people? *After Tears* is very much about black life in a world in which racism resulted in poverty

31

mostly experienced by black people, and the consequences of that racism are that first-generation university graduates find themselves under enormous pressure to provide for friends and relatives at home (the 'black tax' I discuss in Chapter 10), even if that student has actually dropped out of university.

Only a reader from Mars could possibly imagine that the works of Mahala, Mhlongo or Mgqolozana are apolitical depictions of race-less human beings. They are not. They are works of fiction rooted in identity politics.

A FINAL THOUGHT

It's pretty obvious, I hope, that since racism refuses to leave us, black writers cannot escape the race motif and identity themes in their works. Because we aren't robots. We are psychological creatures whose writing comes from deep within. And if you grapple with race, then write about race unapologetically. I don't think this means we cannot or do not write about other topics, but the history of racism and the material reality and legacy of that racism explain why we are less inclined to write a wholly apolitical novel or a collection of essays about classical music.

It is often a burden precisely because black life cannot and should not be reduced to preoccupations about race or politics. I have an interest in moral philosophy, literature, music, and I want to devote some of my career to those subjects too. That is why, I guess, *A Bantu in my Bathroom* was not emotionally as challenging to construct as this book has been. That book only contained a small section on race, and the rest of the essays were about 'nonsense': Are rhinos people too? Is unconditional love a bad thing? Why do we laugh when we laugh? and other social comment. It is almost a relief to be able to say to the white accuser who renders you 'race-obsessed', 'SEE! SEE! I don't only write about race!!' That burden is so annoying that I think one reason my manuscript on illness, death and meaning preoccupies me is because of a desperate desire, born of my black skin, to be able to say again, 'SEE! SEE! I don't only write about race!!'

But fuck it, no further meta-reflections from me on why I write about race. If you don't get why racism is still a thing, stew in your wilful ignorance. Or, wrestle with black writing and get to know the lives of people different from yourself. If you're *black* and don't get why racism is still a thing, stew in your wilful ignorance. Or, wrestle with black writing and get to know the lives of people different from yourself.

HOW ARE YOUNG PEOPLE CONNECTED TO
RACISM'S HISTORY?

IS CROSS-CLASS SOLIDARITY IN A DIVIDED
SOUTH AFRICA POSSIBLE?

WHAT ARE THE ROOTS OF (RENEWED) STUDENT
ACTIVISM ON OUR CAMPUSES?

HEARD THE ONE ABOUT YOUNG PEOPLE NOT SEEING RACE?

MY MANY GRAHAMSTOWNS

Earlier this year I visited my alma mater, Rhodes University, in my hometown of Grahamstown, a city born of colonial misadventure. There is, if you open your eyes wide enough, something extraordinary when you revisit geographies you think you know very well. You begin to see things differently; you feel differently too. I was staying at a bed-and-breakfast on campus, right at the top of a hill that is so steep it forced me to lose calories left over from too many years of drinking at Rhodes half my life ago. That long, hard walk up that steep hill rewarded me, however, with a vantage point from where I could see most of campus and the rest of the city with painful clarity.

Grahamstown easily makes the shortlist for a city whose geography is the most representative of apartheid town planning. You can see the boundaries that were designed to keep white, black, coloured and South Africans of Indian origin, from 'mixing'. This little city is no melting pot; other than, sort of, on the High Street in the middle of Grahamstown, where a giant Cathedral stands erect, gloriously towering over the hint of a CBD. Here, there has to be racial mixing, because privilege cannot be sustained without exploitation. Cheap coloured labour on the cash tills of shops that serve the rich are a necessary allowance of fleeting interracial interaction. Otherwise, the privileged would have to start packing their own shopping bags when they came to stock up before retreating to the suburbs reserved for quiet reflection on what to lecture the next day, argue in the High Court, teach at the private schools, or how to throw the best digs party. Whatever their preoccupation, all would be blissfully unaware of what went on in Joza township far away from elite life on the other side.

But, like coffee stains on a carpet that refuse to disappear, the privileged also have to endure the sight of more begging street kids per square metre on Grahamstown's High Street than probably anywhere else in the country. They simply walk around these kids, not acknowledging their humanity, although some people remark on the 'menacing' *existence* of these street kids in letters to the local rag, the *Grocott's Mail*. Even then their existence – as opposed to their humanity – is observed only to be crushed by angry demands that someone sweep away the nuisances from the curbs, especially in anticipation of national arts festival-goers descending on the place at the end of June each year.

Sure, a few black and coloured teachers have now moved into the suburbs, but don't be fooled by this statistical minority getting a taste of whiteness. The city remains an exemplar of apartheid geography to this day.

Casting my eye that day over a divided city geography, I was wearing my hat as an English-speaking writer schooled at Graeme College Boys High in the luscious green suburb of Somerset Heights on the other side of Grahamstown, a cultural marker perfected for over six years at Rhodes University itself, and all of it augmented later at Oxford University where I wore a tuxedo almost weekly for Oxford Debate Union activities aimed at preparing one for public life disconnected from the working class.

But when I visited my cousins and sisters the following day, on the other side of the railway tracks that take you into the heart of the coloured township in Grahamstown, a different geography, but also a different me, revealed itself. Afrikaans-speaking, rooted in a Catholic upbringing, thoroughly working class, and feeding on the nostalgia of a childhood in which my sisters and I were still living with our parents, one who died years ago and the other now living in Port Elizabeth, there was no hint of the Eusebius made at Graeme and tinkered with further at Rhodes and Oxford. I was sitting in my sister's humble RDP house, on a *vlakkie* way beyond Ghost Town, a part of the coloured community that has a look of despair barely kept at bay by the human spirit's refusal to die from gross inequity. But this tenacity should not be mistaken for flourishing.

My sister had asked me beforehand what she should cook and I dared her to try to emulate Mom's roast chicken, chow mein, beet salad and what we called 'fridge pudding', which is an addictive, multilayered pudding with chunks of caramel, chocolate, custard and other decadent ingredients. She did well, shame, but no one cooks like Mom. Still, we laughed, reminisced and gossiped. I got the list of recent dead and how *that* one and his girlfriend refused to take ARVs out of shame but now are buried, and we pored over a photo of an aunt of ours who seemed to be ageing rather rapidly.

Then I returned to 'The Other Nation' of Mbeki's Two Nation lament, at the other side of town, all the way up on a different hill where the 1820 Settlers' Monument stands, and where I delivered, still full from the nostalgia-drenched meal I had eaten earlier, a memorial lecture in memory of Christina Scott, the brilliant science communicator.

Something else happened on this trip. I met and talked to countless students about a protest that had started at the University of Cape Town, archived on Twitter as #RhodesMustFall, and which had now spread to Rhodes as #RhodesSoWhite. The protests at UCT were not only about the removal of a statue of Cecil John Rhodes on campus, although that was the symbolic focus initially. The bigger trigger was the collective experiences of many students of UCT as an untransformed institution, one that remains exclusionary and unjust in many ways, including in what it teaches, how it teaches, and in its institutional habits, like privileging certain bodies over others and staff demographics which betray a pathetic lack of effective effort to recruit black women academics. It was also a demand for greater sensitivity to the feelings of alienation on the part of many students. It was, in effect, an urgent call for institutional reform on the back of compelling testimonies about the struggles of countless students to survive Rhodes University in the face of odious legacies that still linger.

The issues were broadly similar at other campuses, and so the protests at Rhodes University came as a shock to many alumni who recall their Rhodes experience uncritically, imagining our alma mater to have always been inclusive and progressive. Thus, I too experienced Rhodes differently on this trip – as a proud alumnus of an institution I love, but which I no longer love uncritically. The real heroes today are black, and some white, and many of them middle class, students (but not all of them) who have expressed a political consciousness.

Where has this sudden anger and passion for social justice come from when so many self-appointed elders had written off the 'born free' generation as apathetic, uninterested in politics and ahistorical? For more insight into this question, I turned to some of the people more intimately involved and affected.

AN ENCOUNTER OUTSIDE THE LIBRARY

Outside the Rhodes library I met Elethu Duna. We met in the morning, just before I was to leave for the airport in Port Elizabeth and while I was drinking surprisingly good coffee sitting at The Kaif at Rhodes, a place I had come to associate with avoiding lectures rather than good coffee. Or where you have awesome conversations like the one I had with Duna.

Duna is a single mom doing a master's degree in fisheries management. She had never, she told me, experienced as much anxiety and institutional racism as she had at Rhodes. Duna spent many hours in the Rhodes library, not only because she was intellectually curious. She did it, also, to escape from her academic department where the choking stench of untransformed attitudes and habits threatened to snuff out her curiosity and drive. She felt uncomfortable even communicating with some of the people in her department. Duna had been tempted many times to throw in the towel, so as to feel less anxious again, but was forging on with her studies.

Duna was entitled to have her story, her lived reality, accepted as an honest account of what *she* experienced daily. Your reality, if you're a fellow Rhodent, is not the defining reality of all members of the Rhodes Community. Neither was mine. One of the manifestations of unchecked privilege is how we respond to others' experiences of the same geographies we roam. I have little doubt that many Rhodents, especially white alumni, would be shocked by her description of the university. The first test of one's commitment to be in dialogue with someone else is an ability and willingness to hear them, *truly*, as opposed to simply waiting to speak and tell them they are wrong.

I asked Duna if she was excited about the #RhodesSoWhite campaign which, among other things, was serving as an archiving of the experiences of many students at Rhodes, the multiple ways in which each of them did not feel welcome or at home at the university.

But Duna was sceptical about the campaign. She feared it would prove to be a mere moment, rather than being momentous. One of her friends reinforced this by suggesting that the new vice-chancellor, Dr Sizwe Mabizela, was too timid, too reconciliatory; he initially refused to even hear argument on why the name of the university should be changed, even though he recognised other issues that matter on the transformation agenda.

Duna's story reminded me of an experience I had a few days earlier in Johannesburg when I moderated the launch of an excellent new book that speaks to institutional cultures that are insufficiently transformed at our higher education institutions. The book, edited by Rhodes academics Sally Matthews and Pedro Tabensky, is entitled *Being at Home: Racism, Institutional Culture and Transformation at South African Higher Education Institutions*.

My favourite moment at the book event came when a black female sociologist, Associate Professor Grace Khunou, spoke so much truth to stinky institutional power that, despite being the moderator, I happily flicked my fingers, one-handed, with gay abandon, like one might do at a poetry jamming session, in praise of her; in praise of what could only be described as the spectacular performance of a speech act.

With emotion that pierced, she recounted how she had never once in her academic career, as either student or lecturer, ever felt at home anywhere because she was a black woman who was stereotyped and doubted. She was a black woman about whom the worst assumptions were made, and more. She had to run away from one institution to another in search of a home, and again, as she spoke, she was thinking of running again … from UJ … but the problem, the reality, as she pointed out, was that she could not run away from being a black woman. She would not be at home anywhere, not even in a former black institution, she told me afterwards, where her race might simply result in less racial prejudice but wouldn't shield her from gender prejudice. The simple truth was that no institution in our higher education sector could ever, as they now stand, be 'home' for her.

Later, the truth of her experiences were further affirmed by a black student who said that when a black lecturer rolls an 'r', some students – including black students – can be derisive. They take accent, if not race, as an indicator of intelligence and teaching skill. This stuff runs deep. It is black and white; and yet it also intersects with class, race, gender and other irreducible elements of our identities that cannot be disaggregated as neatly as we often expect, myself included.

Yet again, as painful as Khunou's testimony was of the ways in which some bodies and some identities are privileged over others, her entire being and intellectual activism, in that moment of her testifying, spoke to the kind of political pushback against dominant cultures that Duna – a much younger female intellectual – would reveal to me a few days later down in Grahamstown.

WAITING TO EXHALE

It is interesting that so many black students and black academics, including some relatively privileged ones, are now exhaling. They are owning the ways in which they feel and experience the effects of institutionalised and interpersonal racism on our campuses.

I think one reason is simply that many young black professionals, black students who might have gone to former whites-only schools or private schools, and black academics are fed up with the hierarchy of victimhood in society. I remember, for example, feeling forever grateful as a schoolkid to be attending Graeme College and, later, Rhodes and Oxford. This gratitude made it hard for me to voice the ways in which I was not at home in these spaces. After all, Dad was 'sacrificing' to pay high school fees, and I had a shot at an excellent, life-changing education, which my sisters and cousins did not have, so I should surely just shut up and appreciate that opportunity. Yes?

If you are the first person in your family to have escaped poverty, and you are confronted with this luck every time you go home, you start feeling survivor's guilt. You survived poverty; others didn't, so count your blessings. Enduring the condescending look of white students if you are a black female sociology professor walking into the first lecture you're about to give at UJ seems like a small price to pay for not working the cash machine at Checkers on High Street in Grahamstown, and so you grin and bear it, telling yourself that you need to keep things 'in perspective'.

But, as has been the case with sociologist Grace Khunou, the pressure builds up and eventually you just have to exhale. It is your turn to tell your story of how the continued reality of anti-black racism affects you, even though you may be part of the intelligentsia, the academy, a privileged student with a middle-class background, or presumed to be middle class on account of being a student. And, to be clear, the vast majority of students affected by food insecurity, financial exclusion, linguistic apartheid and inadequate support structures to complete their studies are poor students, mostly poor black students. But it is fascinating that not only poor students were taking part in these protests on our campuses. Racism is so insidious that it doesn't discriminate between poor blacks and middle-class blacks. The black body is a site of hatred regardless of what other privileges intersect a *particular* black body.

It was just a matter of time before middle-class blacks voiced their experiences that they had very often kept to themselves. So one really shouldn't be surprised by the kind of academic activism that you find from UCT academic Dr Xolela Mangcu, Dr Adekeye Adebajo who runs the Centre for Conflict Resolution, and UCT psychology lecturer Dr Shose Kessi. I would also mention UCT academic Dr Siona O'Connell who wrote a newspaper column about the lack of black professors at her institution.[2] O'Connell received a barrage of abuse and threats as a result of expressing her opinion, so much so that an online website that reported on the abuse and ostracisation she experienced had to close its online comments section below the article to minimise, at least on its website, further abuse of her rights to dignity and free speech.[3] O'Connell had received over 800 threatening emails and abusive telephone calls. And what prompted this? Her simply pointing out facts: that by 2013, out of 1 045 academics at UCT, only 48 of them were black, and there was not one single black African woman who was a full-time professor. So being a black academic or a black professional more generally doesn't make you immune to the effects of structural, institutional and interpersonal racism.

Racism follows us everywhere; it doesn't just feature in the lived experiences of poor black people. And while, no doubt, the double horror of racism and poverty make life for poor black people particularly dignity-impairing, I'm not sure if a callous discussion about whether the racism experienced by the poor is worse than the racism experienced by professionals, is worth hammering out. Racism is our common enemy, and while sporadic middle-class-led protests do not yet tell us whether middle-class people will finally understand the many ways in which our fate is tied up with the fate of the poor, the

2 http://www.iol.co.za/capeargus/what-uct-s-not-telling-their-first-years-1.1806441#. VRpSrvmUeW5

3 http://www.iol.co.za/news/south-africa/western-cape/uct-lecturer-ostracised-after-column-1.1824551#.VRpSavmUeW4

possibility for greater cross-class solidarity in pursuit of the total elimination of racism in society should excite anyone with a
genuine interest in justice.

INTELLECTUAL ACTIVISM

This strategic cooperation between groups with overlapping
interests but distinct identities – poor blacks, middle-class
blacks, white allies – is not the only cooperation we see emerging in the pushback against racism's haunting presence. The
vertical power relationships between students and staff are
also being flattened, at least on some campuses. There is little
doubt that academics like Dr Richard Pithouse and Dr Vashna
Jagarnath at Rhodes University do not see themselves only as
academics, researchers and lecturers. Like US philosophy professor Lewis Gordin, who has written extensively on race and
racism, Pithouse and Jagarnath see the academic space as a social and political reality in which social justice must be attained
and experienced by everyone who enters. They are activist
teachers and academics who do not see themselves as gurus
writing truths on the blank minds of ignorant students. They
learn from their students, they are in dialogue with their students, and they rightly see them as academic peers. One structural effect of this approach to pedagogy is that, like Kessi and
O'Connell at UCT, they have been fully supportive of students
who have protested the legacy of racism in the academy. And
this relationship between black academics, progressive white

academics, white students who get it, and black students and black staff, is a beautiful example of the kind of strategic cooperation that ought to unite individuals and groups who have common interests more often than has been the case in democratic South Africa.

Indeed, Kessi has done excellent research as an academic, chronicling the lived experiences of black students at UCT, and the ways in which they do not feel at home. The influence of Pithouse and Jagarnath, in turn, on their students is also evident in the quality of intellectual activism from some postgraduate students. All this is unsurprising: if racism is indiscriminate, academics and students who are its victims, and those in solidarity with the victims, will eventually find one another.

There are countless examples of how this cooperation between conscious academics like Pithouse and postgraduate students with a renewed, public sense of justice and history are resulting in new forms of intellectual activism, despite critics like Professor Jonathan Jansen hastily, waspishly, and inaccurately dismissing these students as not 'getting history'.

A first-year politics master's student at Rhodes University, Lihle Ngcobozi, wrote one of the most brilliant interventions in the debate about statues, heritage, institutional identities and transformation that was raging in the first few months of 2015.[4] Her essay, '#RhodesSoWhite – An Insight', was yet another example of intellectual activism among students, students that

---

4 http://www.theconmag.co.za/2015/03/27/rhodessowhite-an-insight/

many of us had written off as ahistorical, post-race and uninterested in realpolitik, students who simply wanted to get on with making the country a beautiful place unconnected to a jarring past, a place in which racial identities were already discarded.

I quote Ngcobozi at length:

'There has been much backlash against the social media campaign #RhodesSoWhite, which I started on a thread on the Rhodes SRC Facebook page. The rationale behind the social campaign was to expose the collective mental violence faced by black students at Rhodes University on all levels. The backlash this campaign has generated exposes not only how white students are (wilfully) blind to the safety net created for them by being the embodiment of social, cultural, political and economic capital that comes from white normativity. It also exposes how white students on this campus still believe in the trope that racism is racism only if you are grotesquely overt in your disdain for black people.'

She continues:

'The very methodology of racism and the upholding of white supremacy works to distract the black political project of constituting and claiming black subjectivity. This, in and of itself, is the working of anti-black racism, which has unapologetically found itself comfortable enough to claim its space on the Rhodes [Facebook] SRC page and, by and large, [among] a number of white students on campus. Additionally, this social media campaign has also revealed the problematic logic of transcendence as a means of avoiding the discomfort of race. Many students are of the belief that South Africa is in [a] post-racial era where race and racism are things we should get over. This transcendence is an attempt to banalise and conceal race and racism, to depoliticise history and its legacy while delegitimising the process of redress and restoring the dignity of those violently dispossessed. It is important to locate transcendence as avoidance within the national discourse of race among South Africans (white or black). In doing so, we are able to insert the particularities found in our universities into the national conversations of avoidance, denialism and erasure.'

Pause here. If that was hard to get, re-read it. Go back to the previous two paragraphs and grapple with the excellence of a young black South African woman. We grapple with obscure texts by long-dead white European men, and see such grappling as worthwhile intellectual pursuit. Go back and play with, and think hard about, every word in the previous two paragraphs. I will not mediate for a black woman whose brilliance shines without needing me to mansplain her. And then come back, and continue with me: how on earth can anyone read an intervention of this kind as anything other than the meeting point of academic rigour and deep, personal testimony? This is the kind of justice-sensitive academic we found in the white body and person of Ruth First. Anyone who hastily dismisses student leaders like Ngcobozi and accuses them of 'not getting' history or of being distracted from their studies, is just embarrassing themselves because that kind of response reveals a basic lack of rigour on the part of the critic rather than the student. A rigorous critic reads and listens actively to those he or she is in dialogue with, and those they claim to be engaging critically. Whatever your thoughts on issues such as a statue of Cecil John Rhodes remaining or being toppled, it is surely disingenuous to imagine that a bunch of naughty kids too lazy to think or study are leading these debates and protests. Anything but: these protests, as is evident in the academic talent at work in the passages I just cited, are an important demonstration that racism is class-blind and, related, that the black middle class, the black intelligentsia, and black students, are less likely to be toppled than monuments to colonial evils are likely to fall.

Ngcobozi leaves us with the following:

'The presence of the Black Students Movement (BSM) and their call for transformation at Rhodes has challenged the myth of the university having an apathetic and apolitical student body. The BSM has also exposed how, in an attempt to quell the fears of bogeymen alumni who will disinvest from a transformed Rhodes, the institution will label the organising of these students as a "racist storm". A letter sent to alumni, with the title "VC acts swiftly to avoid racist storm at Rhodes", showed how, in an attempt to scramble for the now exposed and shattered myth of Rhodes being a home for all, the BSM movement will be read as racist. This was done to avoid self-critique and reflection on why Rhodes's culture has not transformed even with the change in demographics. The letter and the barring of students of the BSM on March 24 [2015] from the administration building are important messages being sent to these students – that the institution will protect itself from those who wish to disrupt its culture. Although the doors were finally open because the students [insisted] on reading their memorandum inside the building, it speaks to the reluctance of the institution to transform. The doors to transformation will not be open unless those who demand it are persistent in their resolve.'

And:

'These conversations and forms of resistance from the students at the University of Cape Town and the challenging of the presence of historical artefacts of colonial violence should not be reduced to a removal of a statue, the changing of the name of Rhodes University, or social media campaigns. These are all entry points into broader concepts of transformation and black students laying claim to space, and the right for their space to be reflective of a transforming institution. When students call for "Rhodes must fall"

and rally behind #RhodesSoWhite as a collective, we ought
to look deeper into the cause and align ourselves with any
movement that vehemently rejects the untouchable nature
of white normativity and its hold on shaping the experiences of black students at Rhodes, UCT and society at large.'

The BSM is a direct refutation of the myth that only South
Africans around the age of 35 or older have memories of racism, or racial identities. The observation, furthermore, that
'the doors to transformation will not be open unless those who
demand it are persistent in their resolve' is an example of not
seeing academic excellence as an end in itself, but seeing academic excellence as most useful if it changes the world in meaningful ways, and in Ngcobozi's case that would mean a more
just world. It fills my liberal egalitarian heart to know that the
uncritical love that 'liberal' institutions like Rhodes University
and the University of Cape Town have been enjoying is being
disrupted so timeously by students who have a deeper sense
of justice, history and activism than many students from my
cohort displayed when we were there, myself most definitely
included.

And then we lie to ourselves about an apathetic black middle
class, or students who do not know *and experience* the history
of the country they – we – live in. Clearly, it was just a matter
of time before they found their voices. Before they exhaled. No
doubt tens of thousands of these students have not found this
kind of passion displayed by Lihle Ngcobozi. We shouldn't be

hasty about a sea change in attitude among students as an overall collective, but only the worst pessimist would deny that a fundamental shift in how students and academics see their role and place in our society, especially black students and academics, is possible. And that ultimately makes for a more engaging kind of democratic citizen.

SOME CONCLUDING THOUGHTS

It is important to both affirm the identity politics of middle-class black students, and to reflect on its limitations. A few months ago I found myself, most unfortunately, sitting next to an older white woman who has for years run a right-wing economics think-tank in Johannesburg. We were talking about the student protests across our campuses and she managed to irk me by being highly dismissive about the activism of middle-class black students.

She suggested that the stories emerging from rich black kids who went to a private school and who thought a few snide remarks about their hair from a white teacher in high school was a form of 'hair policing', were completely self-indulgent and ill-placed when all around us 'the country is burning!' She suggested that there were more important issues to be grappling with at this point in our democracy than having to listen to privileged black students pretending to be deeply wounded.

I was pissed off, and despite the occasion – a dinner hosted by an ambassador from another country – decided I was not there to affirm the world view of people who think they understand the lives of others and yet have made little effort to achieve any real understanding of those lives. And so I gave her a thorough and audible rebuttal of what I considered an anti-intellectual and rude response to some very important, nuanced and legitimate writing and activism from many students this year, including black middle-class students.

If you are not a black woman who has experienced certain kinds of exclusions and, yes, even violence, then you need to listen with some humility to those women's stories of their daily lived reality. It does not mean it is compulsory to agree with all the analysis and implications of some of the writings and praxis that might emerge, but you are not in a position to arrogantly dismiss the pain of people whose lives you have spent no time getting to know.

Likewise, it is important to push back against attempts to caricaturise the identity politics of some of our young people, caricatures that often come from older South Africans who probably do not want to own up to the fact that the pain of younger people is evidence of older people not having been the trailblazers and leaders many had thought they were.

At one point the woman had the audacity to nearly shout, 'I am not saying they can't feel certain emotions but at some point the university space must be about evidence and facts, about rational argument and not just feelings!'

I referred her to my forthcoming essay in this collection about the moral and instrumental value of emotion and exhibiting emotion, as well as the lie that rules of engagement that are 'rational', completely fair and value-neutral devices are necessary to negotiate conflict and engage in debate. I also told her about the academics and students I had met, including those in this collection, who are academically brilliant, and who serve as proof that emotion and emoting do not crowd out the capacity for rational argument. I suggested that one might realise this only if one did not make assumptions about such activists, but actually read and listened to them closely instead.

By now, I think we had both accepted that we could not persuade the other. My fellow dinner guest sheepishly exited our conversation and struck up a chat with a more agreeable fellow to her left. It was awkward, but there was no way I was going to feed the self-satisfied view that there is no substance in the methodologies and politics of black middle-class student activists.

That dinner table was not, as you can imagine, the place where I would have wanted to go further to discuss the limitations of some of this student activism, because I was with people who might have abused my own critique of some black middle-class students. They were the sort of folks who might ignore the paragraphs preceding this one and quote out of context what I am nevertheless about to say by way of critical reflection.

Our desire to show solidarity with poor and indigent black South Africans – as black middle-class people – is commendable. And overdue, in fact. This cross-class solidarity is appropriate because institutional and interpersonal racism do not give a damn about your bank balance, where you live or what education you have. But, having said that, we are still very privileged as middle-class black people. And I think it is important to check our own privileges rather than potentially monopolising public articulations of the effects of anti-black racism.

I really hate competitions over who can articulate the worst kind of wounds suffered. And so I want to be clear that I do not think, unlike the person who sat next to me at that dinner, that we must trivialise a black professional's experience of racism, for example. All racism is inherently violent and degrading. Yet, despite this truth, it is of course easier to live in this racist world if you are middle class than if you are working class or completely destitute. I am sitting typing this essay in my flat in Sandton while some of my relatives are worried about where dinner will come from. If I take my stated solidarity with the poor and indigent seriously, then the politics of identity that privileges my journeys in white institutions over those of the truly worst off, must engage with class analysis and structural analysis more generally. Black people are diverse because, although anti-black racism unites us, we also experience the world through other social markers, especially class differences between us as blacks.

I do not think that this means black students who have relative privilege compared with poorer black students must switch off the tap from which their pain is pouring, or recede into the background on campuses. That would be the wrong conclusion to infer from the reality that poor blacks are worst off.

There is no genuine choice to be made between 'identity politics' and 'class analysis'. They are not incompatible ways of analysing this troubled society of ours. Indeed, they complement each other by foregrounding the multiple legacies of colonialism and racism. But the caution, however, is that those of us who are middle class must not be complacent about just how much more work we need to do to genuinely understand the minutiae and reality of poverty. Poverty is not our daily reality. And having poor family members does not suffice to make you a grassroots activist for the poor. We need to check the privilege of having escaped poverty.

As I meditated on the issues explored here, I kept feeling guilty. I kept wondering, 'What will my white friends say?' I actively critique white liberals in this collection – arguing that they are not immune to racism or unearned privileges, and that they should engage each other on how to respond to their unearned privileges instead of asking black mates, 'What DO you want from me?!' (I deal with this in more detail later.) In addition, they have to engage a meditation on what might seem like the radicalisation of the black middle-class, black academics and, horror of all horrors, young black people who were supposed to have no racial identities.

I do not know what to make of my own guilt, to be frank. I think I shouldn't feel this guilt but, of course, we don't choose what we feel. But here's why, at least upon reflection, my feelings of guilt about any discomfort white readers may feel are misplaced. The struggle for gender equity provides, again, helpful insight here. A woman who does important feminist work ought not to feel guilt at skewering both grotesque misogyny *and* men who are not overtly misogynist but who benefit from the unearned 'privilege' of a penis in a world structured in ways that benefit males. No doubt many progressive men in the life of that feminist, be they friends, colleagues or family members, may feel very anxious or angry even when they read a trenchant meditation on an aspect of gender activism. But the true test of the commitment of male allies in the fight to eliminate misogyny is whether they can park their exceptionalism and accept that overall structures and patterns in society cannot be dismantled if every and all expositions of gender injustices *must* first and foremost be acknowledged. Nor is it necessary to first placate those men who self-identify as feminists.

Similarly, a white liberal who gets mortally upset that black professionals, black students, and black academics suddenly exhibit and voice anger and confess to feeling like racial aliens in the academy, corporate South Africa, and even in civil society, must chin up. No, really. This has to be about the victim, and not about you, the assistant. A failure to understand this, and come to terms with it, is evidence of precisely what I argue elsewhere: whiteness featuring even in the politics of those whites who imagine themselves to be very different from outright racists. My guilt about causing progressive whites some discomfort persists, I assure you, but then again I was raised Catholic before I had the freedom to crack that religious chestnut as a student. Guilt haunts me occasionally.

It would help, however, if white friends, colleagues and allies of racial justice properly reflected on the need to be comfortable with feeling alienated *themselves,* alienated by black people who previously had kumbaya relations with them, many who now even renounce their English names, reclaiming African identities that were choked in traditionally white institutions. If you feel such alienation from your black pals, welcome to what is the daily discomfort for Elethu Duna, Grace Khunou, Shose Kessi, Xolela Mangcu, Vashna Jagarnath, Adekeye Adebajo, and many other black people in a country where black bodies are a numerical majority.

Here's a dirty, horrid secret: the reason many of us 'coconuts' never made you uncomfortable *before* is because we parked parts of our own identities at home when we came to school, university and the workplace. Or, we didn't park them; we simply hid them in your presence.

Another thought has been tugging at me. Black middle-class people often get more upset when we are let down by white liberals than by outright, right-wing, textbook-variety white racists. We also worry more about what white liberals will think of our ideas. Why is that? 'Moderate' whites get close scrutiny in this collection; right-wing types that are nakedly racist only make fleeting appearances. And the approval of liberal whites secretly matters for many black middle-class people.

One friend of mine, far too bloody clever to be wasted on a

career in law but stuck in one, suggested that we expect more from 'progressive' whites because we know them better, have often benefited from being in relationships with them, and want the love to continue. Any realisation that some of these trusted friends, mentors, sponsors, benefactors, mentees and colleagues are not immune to the ideology and norms of whiteness, hurts. We never had such expectations of members of the Afrikaner Weerstandsbeweging, for example, and so naked, even physically violent, racism from those quarters does not surprise us, or disappoint us.

In fact, even a commentator like Andile Mngxitama, well known for his bruising critiques of white people and blacks friendly with white people, sometimes seems to come close to praising racists who are overt about their hatred of black people. It is almost as if he is relieved that there is no pretence among the likes of Afrikaner activists Dan Roodt, Steve Hofmeyr and Sunette Bridges. While all dominance rooted in racism rightly angers Mngxitama, I suspect he has more time for, say, Roodt and Bridges than he might for politicians like Helen Zille or writer Max du Preez – both of whom are considered 'progressive'.

We are, in turn, disappointed that the memory of schooling together has not guaranteed the complete elimination of whiteness from all white liberals; and, for some of us, there is also a deep disdain for the fake liberal who lacks the guts of the naked racist. All racists, out or in the closet, are disgusting; but it is easier to challenge Roodt than an English-speaking white liberal seen toyi-toying at a political rally in a township.

With the new intellectual activism among young black South Africans surprising us in 2015, these discomforts will not linger for much longer. They will be dealt with and lanced, like the legacy of Cecil John Rhodes. The year 2015 is spectacular testimony to active young citizenship, and the overshadowing of lazy elders whose time has expired.

HOW DO I KNOW I HAVE ENCOUNTERED RACISM?

WHAT GOES ON IN THE HEART OF THE RACIST?

**WHAT'S THE RELATIONSHIP BETWEEN
THE RACIST AND HER VICTIM?**

REPORTING FROM THE RACIST'S HEART

Isn't it amazing that a phenomenon as common as racism can still be poorly understood by us? I think we can all recognise, for the most part anyway, outright examples of racism, like someone beating up another person and explicitly hurling racial slurs at them while doing so, and it being clear that they are in part motivated by racial hatred in their attack on that person.

But we don't have the same kind of consensus about less clear-cut cases. Was Kuli Roberts racist when she wrote a column about coloured women wearing curlers and nighties the whole day, and other stereotypes crammed into a column about this group, a column that saw her fired? If I crack a joke about white people not being able to dance, is that a racist remark? What about a white, Afrikaans foreman who has never hurled racial slurs at his workers, yet speaks to them only in Afrikaans and whose interaction with them is on his terms only – is this mere economic power play or is it overlaid with racism? Where does unearned privilege and unconscious bias end and racism begin?

I've been wrestling these unclear examples of racism since *A Bantu in my Bathroom* was published. The account of racism I developed in that book wasn't far-reaching enough. I focused on racist actions and described these essentially as arbitrary and irrational acts of discrimination on the basis of race. That's not wrong. But it is a definition that only picks out a portion of the racism in our midst. And while I hinted in *A Bantu in my Bathroom* at the relationship between one's *character* and one's *actions*, the focus was mainly on racist actions.

Sadly, racism is far worse than I implied. It would be bad enough if all we needed to worry about were racist actions. But racism isn't restricted to *what we do*. Racism is also, intimately, about *who we are*.

The central distinction here is one that would be familiar to someone who studied philosophy. It is a distinction, however, that deserves discussion beyond academic philosophy because it will help us understand why racism isn't restricted to what we do; why racism, in other words, is also about who we are.

Philosophers draw a distinction between actions and character. If we cut through complex philosophical terrain, we can still borrow the fundamental insights from this distinction without getting lost in the academic detail. Actions refer to doing – anything from a mundane activity like typing on a keyboard to more complex actions like riding a bicycle or dancing at a club. Character, on the other hand, isn't easily observed. I can think of my character as who I am 'on the inside' – a mix of many things including principles that define me and which form the basis from which I tend to act, beliefs, attitudes, behavioural dispositions, etc. The easiest way to reveal who I am – what my character is – is to perform actions that show the world, out there, who I am on the inside.

I'll return to this distinction in a bit. The main aim of this essay is to reflect on the true nature of racism, and to suggest that racism has seeped into the character of the racist even when we do not see the racist performing racist actions. Her racism doesn't function like, say, a light switch: off when turned off, and on when switched on. Racism is really nasty, like a silent killer such as high blood pressure or undetected cancer; it can be in the body, gnawing away at you, even if the signs are not obvious to someone else, or even to yourself.

I am grateful to philosopher Lewis Gordon for helping me see features of racism I had missed or underemphasised before. A couple of delicious encounters with Gordon in Grahamstown and Johannesburg over the past year necessitated this essay. (I'm also grateful to him for the very idea of seeing the world in new ways.) I had missed these features, or grasped them only fleetingly, precisely because of the limits of an analytic approach to life, including the limits of an analytic inquiry into the nature of racism.

I want to tease out three features of racism here: a) motivating why we should prefer accounts of racism that take us into the heart of the racist over ones focusing only or mainly on actions; b) explaining the racist's narcissism; c) exploring the relationship between the racist and her victim.

JOURNEY INTO THE HEART OF THE RACIST

It's worth going back to that earlier distinction between actions and character. Firstly, I definitely do not want to underestimate the moral and legal seriousness of racist actions. Such actions have no place in a decent society. And we are right to be outraged when public acts of racism are reported.

The problem is that we can miss the full racist picture if we stop there. And this is why it is worth asking what else is going on in the head or the heart of the racist. Because chances are that a racist action comes from somewhere, rather than being a random nasty event over which the person who committed it has no control. It is precisely for this reason that we need to ask what kinds of characters, or what kinds of people, *typically* act in a racist manner. And the answer, of course, is that *racist characters typically commit racist actions.*

Now, I am pretty sure many people who have just read the previous paragraph might go, 'Duh!' But actually this is pretty complicated stuff. Remember we defined character as roughly referring to who I am 'on the inside' – principles, beliefs, attitudes, etc. – and if there is a relationship between my 'true' self and the things I do publicly, then we should be concerned not just with our actions but also, in fact, with the kind of people we are privately, and when we are not acting.

I think this is right, and the reason it is hard to make sense of, in part, is because some people think that laws and moral judgements should only be about actions we perform that harm or benefit people, practically. Many people don't like the idea of making judgements about someone's personal make-up, including their thoughts and their attitudes which may not harm other people in any obvious way. So it is quite controversial, some might think, to extend an account of racism from pure actions to include people's characters and psychologies.

But I think this is right, upon reflection. What matters in life is not only what we do but what kind of people we are. This is why Ancient Greek philosophers, for example, are well known for focusing on virtues and vices. I am not for a moment suggesting that we should all start panicking that we are not perfectly virtuous. Flip, that's very hard when doing wrong often feels quite pleasurable, from minor failings like not keeping an appointment to even cheating on your spouse. But what these Ancients were surely right about is that if we are to be a community of morally decent people then we must both work on *our private selves* and think carefully about *our public actions*.

If you are persuaded by all of this, then there are fascinating consequences for racism that follows: *it means that the racist is not only morally accountable for her racist actions; she is, in addition, a moral failure because her character is stained with racism.* This focus on the character of the racist is what takes us from her actions and into her heart where the racism lurks, a motivational force that inspires racist behaviour.

Looking into the racist's heart reveals fascinating dark truths. The racist displays what philosopher Jorge Garcia has called a 'vicious ill-will' towards people who look differently to her. This captures the psychology of racism in a way that one can miss, or underemphasise, if you focus mostly on actions. It is an attitude of *viciousness* towards other races that is structured into the will of the racist.

What is particularly powerful and surely persuasive in this depiction from Garcia is that one can imagine a 'vicious ill-will' taking root in my character and looking for opportunities to reveal its racist poison. And 'viciousness' in this context points to a serious character flaw, a moral failing, a vice. And, like all vices (and virtues), viciousness is something that becomes part of my character after much practice. It is habit. So the racist is someone who is *in the habit* of looking for opportunities to show off her ill will towards other race groups. There is, in other words, something enduring about her racist character, enduring over time and across space and location.

And by the way, this expanded account of racism doesn't mean that the racist will now be let off the hook because 'character' seems to be something we are born with, you might think. If we look at part of someone's character, like personality traits, you may think it is a matter of luck whether someone is a nice guy or a real asshole, patient or impatient, able to pay attention to detail, or very chilled about getting things precise, etc.

I am no biologist but I do have an intuition that our genetics play some role, presumably, in shaping who we are as people, including our characters and not just physical attributes. However, that said, bad habits can be unlearned with enough effort and practice, just as good habits can be formed with enough effort and practice. And if part of the story of someone's racism includes bad habits they have formed which are now moulded into their character like glue between two pieces of wood, then she must chip away at that glue so that it can loosen and even fall off one day.

So, focusing on the character of the racist doesn't let her off the hook as if she were some kind of natural disaster. But it does mean that if we want to eliminate racism fully and finally from society, we must know that we have our work cut out for us: racism is so widespread that it includes not only overt public acts of racism but in addition includes poisonous racist characters all around us that endure over a very long time, looking to strike, when opportunities for racism come about.

THE RACIST IS A NARCISSIST

Lewis Gordon brought narcissism's role in racism to my attention.[5] We explored what goes on when a white racist is surprised when a black person is appointed to a job for which the racist had also applied. One possibility, of course, and one that is quite typical in South Africa, is that the racist assumes that the black appointee is, in reality, incompetent and probably just a beneficiary of race-based affirmative action.

Gordon pointed out that, invariably, more lurks here. The racist also assumes that they are obviously, and inherently, more qualified for the job that they did not get. It is something of a self-evident truth for the racist that they are better than

---

5 https://soundcloud.com/eusebius_mckaiser/eusebius-in-conversation-with

their black competitor for the job. There is a failure here to even conceive of the *possibility* that, in fact, they were not awarded the job because they are not as good as a black person. This is the essence of the racist's narcissism.

The object of their surprise and disappointment is not only the success of the supposedly incompetent, undeserving black person. There is, simultaneously, a self-reflexive feature at work here: a belief in one's brilliance, one's superiority over black bodies. The racist deeply admires her own attributes, which are obviously, in her egotistical world, perfect, and if not perfect, certainly inherently better than traits a black person might have. That is why they are shocked, disappointed, surprised when they do not get the job. Because they are consumed by a narcissism that blocks reflection, let alone inquiry, into the facts of the particular case.

It could turn out that the black candidate was indeed undeserving; that they were a beneficiary of race-based affirmative action; and even that the racist is infinitely more skilled and fit for the job. But these are open questions of fact that do not even interest the racist. They do not wish to make an inquiry like an intellectually and morally honest person would, before bitching about an injustice they suffered. The racist's mind is made up about cases like these, regardless of what they might learn if evidence for the decision is presented to them. Narcissism motivates the racist to see the world in a way that affirms their deeply held belief that they are too awesome to be beaten in a job application by a black person.

I delighted and laughed when Gordon explored this feature with me in dialogue on racism. The reason for my delight was simply enjoyment at building a richer account of racism than I had possessed till now, and seeing new things I was blind to before. The reason for the laughter, however, was because the concept of 'narcissism' is not one many of us would seriously entertain outside certain colloquial contexts, like perhaps when we refer to someone who quotes themselves a lot as being, on those occasions, narcissistic. It is important, however, for us to import the concept of 'narcissism' into our account of the details of racism.

I think one reason we often fail to delve into the character traits of racists, and specifically the trait of 'narcissism', is because so often public debate focuses nearly exclusively on the victims of racism. That is important. It is the victims, after all, whose dignity is shredded when they are the object of racist actions. And it is the victim's entitlement to justice – something not yet achieved in South Africa – that deserves to be prioritised in public policy discussion, certainly. But this racism beast is so darn powerful that we cannot afford to pick and choose which of these interrelated conversations we focus on. All of them matter.

At any rate, racism is about both the racist and the victim of racism and this *relationship* cannot be easily untangled.

THE RACIST AND HER VICTIM:
RELATIONAL KNOTS

Some, like Steve Biko, have pointed out that one aim of a non-racist society is that whites learn to overcome their superiority complexes and blacks, in turn, dismantle the inferiority complexes that are part of our psychologies.

As Biko suggests, there is a relational property to racism that is both banal and yet often neglected in discussion about how to reduce racism. Put simply: a hermit could not experience racism, sexism or homophobia, for example. These injustices have to be committed by someone in order for them to be the subject of the injustice. In one sense, of course, this is an obvious truth. But in political strategising about how to deal with racism, differences about strategies often reveal deeper differences between activists, about the importance of this *relational* feature of racism.

For example, well-known South African journalist and *City Press* editor Ferial Haffajee asks, provocatively, what would happen if white people did not exist? Her aim, in part, is to have a conversation with black South Africans about why it is that we often measure ourselves, in what we set out to achieve personally, politically or otherwise, against what white people do, or have done.

A different example, from a radio debate I once hosted, is the following question I posed: should black parents and black learners find ways of changing and owning a new institutional ethos and culture at former whites-only schools or must we get on with building educational institutions that are black-led, started-from-scratch exemplars of excellence independent of what happens at former whites-only schools?

And in the media, one cannot forget deep disagreement years ago about whether or not it was unconstitutional for black journalists to form a professional body that requires one to be black in order to be a member.

These examples point to the political and practical differences we have about how to tackle racism. But if we agree that there is a relational element to racism that is intrinsic to racism then it follows that strategies aimed at reducing the consequences of racism must take account of this relational element. This is not to discard the possibility that some work needs to be done to deal with the inferiority complexes that Biko drew to our attention, and that some of that work can and must be done in blacks-only spaces. Some work can be done in such spaces in the absence of white bodies and white 'thought leaders' and white allies of the struggle against anti-black racism.

Equally, it is worth asking what standards we would set for ourselves in the absence of whites, as Haffajee asks of us. And, sure, educational centres of excellence in black townships are important markers of breaking the inferiority complexes we inherited socially. But if racism is partly manifested as my fear to be fully confident and fully human, in how I see myself in the presence of white people, then it is also crucial, as we complete our account of racism and think about what we want to achieve practically, that we do not lose sight of one of racism's most central features: relationship paralyses between blacks and whites.

It is little achievement for me to be articulate, compelling and carry myself with a sense of dignity – intrinsic dignity I possess by virtue of being human – in the presence of fellow black South Africans if I become a wallflower in the presence of white people. Equally, a white person who can own their unearned privileges, and racism, in dialogue with fellow whites is making progress in chipping away at his or her racist character, but the acid test of that journey out of racism is how that white person behaves in my black presence. That is what it means to take seriously the relational element of the racism beast.

CONCLUDING THOUGHTS

I have in recent months participated in several public events that all tried to take stock of the quality of race relations in South Africa, premised on the intuition that race relations and racism are worse than ever before. But what these public events also included, almost as a matter of course, is the question: 'What should we do?' or 'What are the solutions to racism and poor or impaired race relations in South Africa?'

It is worth remarking on the desire for 'solutions'. In my experience, both in the South African media, in public fora of the kind I had recently participated in, and within the academy, there is a rush to engage the race debate in the form of solution-seeking. This, in my view, is hasty. It is evident that there are deep disagreements about what the past consisted of, how the past has affected the present, and what the nature and scope of racism's nasty presence are, or are not, in contemporary South Africa. Complete consensus on history, and complete consensus on the nature of contemporary social challenges, are not preconditions for making progress in chipping away at structural, institutional and interpersonal problems. What is required, however, is overlapping consensus about the nature and extent of our racism problems, and some consensus about what the ideal South Africa roughly looks like. Absent such overlapping consensus and solution-seeking will be doomed to disappoint.

Solution-seeking is often a symptom of discussants avoiding the work of building an accurate and full account of what racism *is*. It is very important that we first share, as a society, a basic picture of what it is that we are trying to eliminate. But if we do not agree what makes an action racist or when someone can be said to have a racist character, then we can't even begin to look for effective strategies to get rid of racism. Diagnosis must precede prescription.

And so this essay is located inside the diagnostic question. If it turns out that I am more or less right, whatever you think of the details, then we need solutions not just aimed at reducing the incidence of public acts of racism, but also ways in which we can reduce racism in the hearts of way too many South Africans. If we disagree about whether that is the true nature of racism, then we must continue the conversation about racism's characteristics rather than anxiously asking for easy solutions, which do not exist.

**MUST I DEMAND A RACISM RECEIPT BEFORE
I BELIEVE A STORY OF RACISM?**

**IS IT A MISTAKE TO APPLY CRIMINAL LAW
STANDARDS OUTSIDE THE COURTROOM?**

**IS RACISM EXCEPTIONAL OR NORMALISED
IN OUR SOCIETY?**

RACISM RECEIPTS

One of the reasons I never even dared to think that I had been raped as a child is because I wasn't sure I could prove it. Doubt can be doubly disempowering: I didn't just doubt whether other people might believe me but also whether I had enough reason to believe *myself*.

This kind of doubt is so disempowering that you do not even think the thought, 'I was raped'. What could be more disempowering than a doubt that controls your mind when you're alone, not allowing certain thoughts to form? And so when I first thought this unpleasant thought as an adult, it felt mischievous because doubt had been policing my memory since childhood.

I remember when I shared what had happened to me as a child with a university friend. We had enjoyed plenty of wine and had been chatting for several hours, sharing all sorts of uncomfortable but also a few pleasant truths about our pasts. The atmosphere and moment seemed appropriate for opening up. It turned out we had similar kinds of horrid truths from our past.

Looking back on that conversation from the late 1990s, it's clear to me now that two things mattered to me in that moment: having my story affirmed rather than being doubted; and feeling a weird kind of security knowing that the person had experienced something similar and that I could take for granted the fact that they genuinely believed me.

But imagine, as absurd and even callous as the thought might be, that I got a receipt as a victim of sexual violence which I could keep and produce every time I doubted myself or someone else doubted me? Imagine that some authority – maybe a doctor or a social worker or a team of health professionals – examined me as a kid and, having concluded I was a victim, issued me with a receipt for the violation.

An exciting new voice in social discourse in South Africa, Danielle Bowler, fresh from completion of an excellent master's thesis on coloured identity, introduced me to the very useful idea of receipts-politics.

Of course that would be a weird world to live in. One tragic advantage of such a receipt is that it might help me to respond effectively to people who think I am a liar, who think I am looking for attention and so have made up a sordid story. Or I could show the receipt to the rapist if he denies it, complete with dates that match a time when he was alone with me, supposedly looking after me while my parents were at a function in town.

In the real world, however, there are no receipts for wrongdoing. We are violated and often just carry memories with us through the rest of our lives. If we were harmed physically also, we might have some physical scars, but there is no real proof that you experienced the violation. You know you did. And your perpetrator knows you did. In the unlikely event there were eyewitnesses, they too know. You all know this without receipts having been issued but there is no tangible proof.

Yet we live in a complex social world where evidence is important. We can't jail your rapist if we do not have evidence that he raped you. And not just any evidence will do; the evidence needs to show beyond reasonable doubt that he is guilty. In a sense, the court demands that you show it receipts for the rape. No receipts, no guilty verdict.

It's not just victims of sexual violence who get routinely doubted, but also victims of other forms of oppression, including racism. One of the most unfortunate symptoms of this systematic doubt that racism is real is when someone who reports an experience of racism is told that they are 'playing the race card'. This is not even a demand for a racism receipt. It is actually worse. It is a refusal to simply accept that a genuine instance of racism might be reported. At least the person who demands proof of racism is open to potential persuasion that we have a real case of racism before us.

Still, this kind of language – 'playing the race card' – indicates a climate in which victims of racism are expected to doubt their memory or are invited to accept that they are just plain wrong about what they think they experienced. They need to 'get over race' and 'stop thinking everything is about race'.

If racism receipts were issued, of course, then racism's victims might have an easier time being believed when they report an experience of racism. In the real world, however, there are victims of racism but no racism receipts. Yet, as with sexual violence, perpetrators can't be dealt with legally unless we have proof, unless we have racism receipts.

This raises the central question of this essay: given that evidence matters in our world (and for good reasons, as I explore shortly), how do we square the importance of proof that someone did something wrong with the social reality that some experiences are so commonplace that it is absurd and insulting to demand receipts for them?

I want to argue that we can sometimes assume that racism was experienced until we have reason to believe otherwise. Yes, that means I am prepared in some circumstances, in the current South African context, to assume that someone is guilty of racism until proven innocent.

But don't be fooled, please, by the language I am using for purposes of stating my view upfront. When I say I am prepared to think of someone as guilty of racism until proven otherwise, I don't mean this legally. It is important to distinguish the demand for racism receipts *in a court of law* from what happens *outside the courtroom.*

Outside the courtroom I think we need different standards to decide when to regard someone as a racist. We should not use legal standards uncritically in our social discourse and in moral life. There might, in other words, be good legal reason to find someone not guilty of racism in a court of law, and yet, in the court of public opinion, we could still be justified in finding him guilty of racism, judge him morally, and even ostracise him socially.

In order to understand what I mean by this distinction between legal standards and life outside the courtroom, a good starting point is to look broadly at sexual violence, criminal law and the court of public opinion, before returning more specifically to the issue of racism receipts.

SHOULD WE DEMAND RAPE RECEIPTS FROM BILL COSBY'S ALLEGED VICTIMS?

Before you drop your mug of coffee in fear of an answer that could open me up to successful legal action for ruining a damaged reputation, no, of course I do not know as a matter of fact whether allegations of sexual predation, including rape and sexual assault, against this comedy legend are true. No one, without definitive evidence, can say that the statement 'Bill Cosby is a rapist' is true or false.

But consider a different question. Can you ever be justified *in assuming* that anyone is a sexual predator or rapist? I certainly think so. And it is crucial to explain the difference between the requirements for legal conviction, and standards required for non-legal judgements. Despite my love of legal debate, and being a Legal Theory major, I think we obsess way too much about legal standards when we discuss and debate social and political issues. It is necessary to get a proper grip on the importance and role of legal standards and how they differ from other standards in society that play a different kind of role in our social lives.

There are different standards in the law itself. You can win a civil case on a balance of probabilities, but you won't be found guilty of a crime unless the state proves beyond reasonable doubt that you committed it. 'Balance of probability' and 'beyond reasonable doubt' are two different evidential standards that operate in the law. And though 'beyond reasonable doubt' is a higher burden of proof than 'balance of probability', they are both quite high burdens to meet when you compare both standards with what we do outside of the courtroom in our daily interactions with one another.

If I meet a stranger at the bar and listen to his thirty-second interaction with the barman, I routinely in such situations make judgements about character, thinking such thoughts as 'What a prick!' or 'Geez, aren't we Mr Nice Guy ... what a gent!' We might be tempted to say that we misspeak in everyday language, that is, that we don't really mean to judge someone on the basis of such thin evidence.

That would be a lie, though. We do form character judgements quite quickly. It is a fact of social life that we do so. And, frankly, we do so for good reason: you cannot – it's just bloody impossible – spend hours, let alone days and weeks, with every stranger you come across before you make a judgement about them. Dare I say, just to get through the day, you probably have to trust your gut about people, without decisive evidence, based on certain cues.

But you could be mistaken, of course. That prick might end up at your table, being mates with one of the people at the table, and that prick could have a chat with you for five minutes and you could change your initial view of him.

Here's the point: it is reasonable, on the basis of a wealth of stored, daily experiences, for you to make assumptions about the prick, until you have reason to think otherwise. You are not, in my view, committing a huge sin judging the guy based on the interaction you witnessed at the bar. After all, you are open to changing your mind later when you learn more about him. So you are happy to revise your judgement, but for the moment it is your assumption that he is a prick, and it is a good working assumption because he fits the profile of countless pricks you've seen behave like that at the Rat and Parrot bar counter in Grahamstown.

If you never met the prick again after that initial bar counter meeting, would a court of law have agreed that you are right to label him 'prick' if we assume for fun that it is criminal to be a prick? Of course a court would not agree with you. You would never have met the high burden of 'beyond reasonable doubt' – even a mediocre lawyer would have you for breakfast under cross-examination about the flimsy evidential basis of your claim. But thank God you don't have to worry about legal standards when you are clubbing. I cannot even imagine what a weird night out you would have if you only formed judgements on the basis of legal standards.

This doesn't mean the law is silly. The reason why the evidential standard in a court of law is so high is that a lot is at stake. You could be thrown into jail if you're found guilty of a crime. Your freedom of movement would be taken away. In any country where the death penalty is legal, you could even be lawfully killed by the state. And all of this in addition to a ruined reputation that could haunt you even after society punished you for breaking the social contract. I'm very glad that legal standards are not child's play. They are the only way to balance the law's regulatory purpose with the fact that we do not want the law to punish people willy-nilly. Legal standards are a good thing in society.

But there is absolutely no reason at all why these legal standards must apply in all aspects of our lives. Not much is at stake if I think you are a prick. It is my private thought. You are not harmed. In a worst-case scenario it might mean I decide not to compliment you on having awesome biceps, as I so intended when I got to the bar, but now don't feel like flattering a prick. These are minor consequences of thinking badly of you. And that is why forming such judgements is not the end of the world; if I get it wrong, not much turns on that for me or you. And if I get it right, I avoided wasting time striking up a chat with someone who is a nasty person. So a lower evidential bar in that kind of context is fine, and I would even add, necessary, given the time constraints under which we act in countless daily situations. Life's too short to be a lawyer when trying to decide whether to go home with Louise that night. Make a quick call and cut your losses if the redhead was actually a missed opportunity because you misjudged her.

This brings me back to sexual predation and rape receipts. If someone is accused by, let's say, twenty different women of sexual assault, I think it is reasonable for us to assume that he did it. This would not be reasonable in law, for excellent reasons to do with why courts demand a higher evidential standard, as I have just explained.

But let's add a couple of facts to this hypothetical case. Assume most of these women have never met, and do not know one another. Add to that the fact that just by making such an allegation each woman will go through various challenges for the rest of her life. You could be tagged, even by those who believe you, as a 'rape victim', 'the woman who was assaulted by so-and-so', etc. These labels often stick, as if the core identity of a survivor is 'rape victim'.

There can also be worse consequences: many people will simply not believe you, and accuse you of trying to ruin a good man, of being after his money, of jealousy, or trying to pretend that you are not, say, 'a whore' when in fact you are a whore and you consented and now cry wolf.

But it gets worse. Not just in the court of public opinion will you be grilled and your reputation defiled; you could find yourself caught up in our adversarial criminal justice system like a plastic bag stuck in a barbed-wired fence. A defence attorney and even a judge could re-traumatise you with misogynist lines of questioning that shred your dignity. One thinks, for example, of one of the women who accused South African tennis legend Bob Hewitt of sexually preying on her when she was his tennis pupil. She recalled him sometimes standing behind her, and teaching her how to hold her racquet for some shots, but she could feel his erect penis against her back.

Imagine the courage a woman needs in order to share in court the detail of what she experienced as a child. What does the defence attorney ask at this stage? Brace yourself: How do you know you were not just feeling a tennis ball in his pocket?

WHAT THE HELL?! Unfortunately, many lawyers care more about the law of evidence – 'beyond reasonable doubt' – than taking care not to traumatise an accused.

And, as I said above, caring about legal standards is a good thing. If Hewitt is sent to jail, the court must be very sure he is indeed guilty of sexual violence and not risk a miscarriage of justice that can ruin his life, a life already compromised on account of the allegations being registered. (As it happens, Hewitt was in fact found guilty.)

But put all of these realities, from the perspective of women, together. If twenty different women who do not know one another, who stand to lose a lot, who are likely to have their sexual histories paraded in court and find themselves subjected to uncaring adversarial justice systems, all decide, against the odds, to assert their personal truth about being survivors of rape, then, given the structural and pervasive nature of violence against women in our society, it seems very bizarre to me that someone would not believe them unless and until a conviction is secured in a court of law.

After all, a court of law may have good reason to dismiss the case, as a matter of *good legal practice*. But what the law cannot do is change social truths about the world we live in. We live in a world, especially here in South Africa, in which women are systemically oppressed, not just through exclusion from opportunities in society, but also domestically and publicly in violent and invasive ways, including rape. This is our shameful reality.

Knowledge of sexual predation runs in our blood; we are soaked in misogynist attitudes and habits. I don't need to have a forensic report about the twenty women to trust their testimony. I am from the same world as them, the world in which I doubted myself because I didn't have a rape receipt.

Of course, there is a chance that all twenty women in this hypothetical case are lying. If we deny that possibility then we would have no evidential standard and that would be absurd. I am not immune to that possibility and would change my assumption that they are telling the truth *when confronted with evidence* that they are lying. The claim I am making is that some lived experiences do not need verification to be believed. The chances of a secret conspiracy among twenty women of different generations, many of whom do not need financial settlements or other possible material benefits that could motivate false allegations, are slim to zero.

The moral isn't that someone cannot lie about being a victim of sexual abuse. The moral is that we should not be swift to assume that they are lying or demand that they show us rape receipts before we take them seriously. That kind of scepticism is unwarranted in a society like ours in which violence against women, and sexual violence in particular, has become normal. Rather be sceptical of the innocence of the alleged perpetrator against whom those victims, with much to lose, have spoken out.

And, in some contexts, you can even assume, in the court of public opinion, that the alleged perpetrator is guilty until you have evidence to prove otherwise. This assumption is reasonable if, for example, there are many victims who speak out, and who have a lot to lose, and little or nothing to gain, and none of whom know of one another but have remarkably similar stories to tell that speak of a believable and familiar pattern of sexual predation.

Don't drag legal norms and standards into every part of daily life.

THE IMPLICATIONS OF RACISM RECEIPTS

So here are the implications then for racism. Someone can reasonably be assumed to be guilty of racism, in some contexts where racism is as common as misogyny, until we have reason to believe they are the exception to the racism motif. That should not shock you unless, of course, you want to deny the pervasive nature of racism in the same way that many deny the structural nature of misogyny.

We become obsessed with exceptional examples of wrongful accusations and do not focus on the general patterns in our society, as if exceptions undercut very familiar, entrenched lived experiences recognisable to most of us.

Some people refuse to even contemplate a racist motive when there is an incident like media reports earlier in 2015 of a school where white boys raped a black boy with a broom. Unless someone – some authority on racism, some scientific guru one presumes – investigates the incident, cuts open the heads of the perpetrators, looks for the part of the head labelled 'motive lives here' and sees a racist motive, and tries unsuccessfully to falsify the observation in further tests to prove racism really was what the guru saw … unless all of this kind of incredibly rigorous work is done, we cannot say anything about the motive of the white boys.

These racism sceptics will only believe me when I say there was a racist motive if I show them a receipt from the racism guru that confirms that racism was indeed found to have been a motivating factor upon scientific investigation.

Well this is just sheer rubbish, and I'll explain why. I am sorry to disappoint fellow men but I am not going to demand of twenty women who accused a powerful man of sexual predation that they show me rape receipts. A judge might do so. And I support that in the context of a criminal trial, sure. I won't ask for receipts if I meet them at a braai, and after a long conversation they open up to me and tell me that they were raped. Because to ask them to show me receipts is to pretend that respect for women is the norm in our society and that misogyny is rare, and that I ought to doubt such claims as a matter of course. The opposite is true: misogyny, not gender equity, is the social norm.

Racism operates in the same way. It is so entrenched in our world that our interactions – interpersonal interactions and those within and with systems in our society – are overlaid and infused with racism. Even the inappropriately named born-free generation inherited these racism memes because they were born into a society that has racism in abundance. It is little wonder that campaigns to remove the images of colonial powers like the statue of Cecil John Rhodes gained so much momentum at the University of Cape Town: racial consciousness is a South African thing, just as much as rainbow myth-making is a South African pastime. Don't tell me to give you receipts to prove lived realities that are commonplace for the vast majority of us who are victims of anti-black racism.

Look, then, at how the gang rape of that black school pupil played out. *Beeld* editor Adriaan Basson, who is an important, progressive ally in the fight to eliminate structural racism, found himself in a social media debate about whether the incident was only a rape incident (and I say 'only' here very uncomfortably in full knowledge that rape is inherently traumatic), or whether it was a violation more *fully* described as 'a sexual crime motivated by racist hatred'. He wasn't willing to describe it as a hate crime against a black person on the basis of race. Basson wanted to be shown racism receipts. Unless the racism guru were to go to that school, cut open the heads of the white boys, investigate their motive, and issue a receipt for racism if their motive is scientifically confirmed to be racism, Basson would not consider that there was racist intent on the part of the boys.

He justified this by saying that in the video that circulated there were boys of different race groups in the room, and although the alleged rapists were white, this racial melting pot in the video is, if anything, evidence that racism isn't a factor here. But at any rate, a racism receipt must be issued before one can say that racism made a cameo appearance at the crime scene. This is laughable. It is as laughable as wanting twenty women to be issued receipts before you believe they were raped.

I laugh off the demand for a racism receipt because I know the society I live in. There is a better chance of me winning the lottery tonight than that a school, focusing on agriculture, in a northern province in South Africa, with an Afrikaans heritage, and a boarding school now featuring black and white kids coming from *our* racist homes, should not have racist memes. A presumption of racism in these familiar structures and locales of racism is justified. Because this is South Africa and not Mars. To demand a receipt for racism is to deny the humongous number of personal daily testimonies of black people about how they experience racism everywhere, including in our schools. Even black academics with access to resources, and who by definition are middle class and have more agency and exit options than a few black teens in a hostel in the middle of nowhere …

91

even they experience institutional racism daily. No receipts are required to know this: racism runs in our blood.

As it happens, some reporters wrote a story that confirmed that there was evidence of racial hatred as a motive. Some pupils, it would seem, were upset by a possible interracial relationship that the rape survivor was in. Basson apologised for his hasty remark that we cannot impute a racist motive, but the apology, though heartfelt, foregrounded the fact that a racism receipt had been issued.

But the sincerity of an apology isn't enough to guarantee its acceptance. Even if one feels like an asshole for critiquing an apology, there are crucial moments in public debate when we need to hit the pause button when an apology is being offered. Basson's apology was undermined by the fact that it was grounded in receipts-politics. He has not accepted (or if he has he has not yet said or demonstrated so) that we live in a country in which, outside a courtroom, it is reasonable in many cases, like the one that played out in that hostel, to assume racism is part of the story of what happened, *even before your reporters are dispatched to the scene*. Unless Basson accepts this as our vicious social reality, his apology doesn't comfort. Because it suggests that if a black worker comes into his office, sobs for ten minutes before he finally speaks, and tells a long story of months of racial abuse at the hands of another colleague, all Basson would presumably say, in addition to listening actively and offering a tissue and a nice bear hug, is, 'I will investigate thoroughly. I promise. And if a racism receipt is issued, I will take STRONG action, Sipho!' He will not say, 'I believe you. Let me follow due process, however, and keep you informed of how it plays out. But I believe you Sipho. Such is the racism our country, and therefore this company of ours too, is founded on. I'm sorry.'

The demand for racism receipts, just like the demand for rape receipts, is simply a refusal to accept that our world is deeply stained by daily violations of human rights that are normal and not exceptional. This denial is further entrenched by pretending that evidential standards in criminal law must also apply in our social lives outside the courtroom. It would be more honest to demand receipts of a virtuous character or of an innocent institution than to demand evidence that our world is a systemically unjust place for women and black people.

**DO MEN NEED WOMEN TO FIGURE OUT HOW TO
DISMANTLE MISOGYNY?**

**IS IT LAZY OF WHITES TO ASK BLACKS HOW TO
UNDO RACISM'S LEGACY?**

**HOW SHOULD I DEAL WITH MY
UNEARNED PRIVILEGES?**

'WHAT *DO* BLACK PEOPLE WANT FROM ME?!'

I am sometimes tempted to feel sorry for white liberals. But the feeling doesn't last for long. The temptation stems from the fact that many white liberals want to be – and many are – allies in the fight against racism, but they are damned if they do something and damned if they don't. If they do nothing, many of us will diss their silence and indifference. On the other hand, if they try to get involved, some of us will tell them either to sit down or take a back seat, inspired by Biko's powerful critique of the overzealous role of the white liberal during the struggle against apartheid.

White liberals aren't enemies. Their resources and good intentions could be harnessed in the pursuit of social justice. And should be. But it remains important, as Biko articulated with clinical insight, to guard against white paternalism – telling black people what to do, leading black people or attempting to do so, *thinking* for black people – and simultaneously to guard against dismissing white people as a matter of course. Mutual recognition isn't possible if there is permanent, mutual and deep distrust.

Biko's position, however, created anxiety among well-meaning whites. And it still does. This is why you will often hear a white person, desperate to make amends, asking of black people what it is that she can do that falls between silence and indifference at one extreme, and overzealousness at the other. This is precisely the focus of this essay: How should black people respond to white liberal anxiety?

'WHAT *DO* BLACK PEOPLE WANT FROM ME?'

Many white South Africans, including some close friends, colleagues, mentors and mentees of mine, want to help make a contribution to social justice. Some of them are also examples of white liberals who often despair, though. If they try too hard (but sincerely so), they get a sense that even black people they had regarded as good friends might come after them, sometimes publicly. They might be accused of not being immune to the vestiges of racism, and whiteness. So it is tempting for them to despair, feeling that their efforts would come to nought anyway.

These white liberals often wonder at some point, 'What DO black people want from me? How can I help? I want to help. TELL ME HOW, PLEASE!' And that's where the temptation to feel sorry for white liberals kicks in. I mean, here is someone, not a racist troll, committed to social justice, and they seem not to have a guaranteed place at the table of black activists and thinkers and social media echo chambers aimed at dislodging hegemony. What is a good whitey to do then? Give up and retreat into a middle-class enclave? Well, I have a few things to say to someone who feels like this, and for whom these questions surface, anxiously, daily.

YOU'RE (STILL) ASKING THE WRONG QUESTION

In *A Bantu in my Bathroom* I told the story of a white stranger who tracked down my number, called me, and desperately pleaded with me to tell him what he could do to make racial amends. He was so anxious and so keen that he said he was willing to learn a local language, and even struck up a conversation with a random black person in a mall in Cape Town where he was roaming about, searching for peace of mind and heart.

I was a bit taken aback and we chatted for a while, but the reality I had to make him aware of is that unearned white privilege is so pervasive that even his attempt to make amends revealed his white privilege. Black people can't just casually walk up to white people in a mall. The white shoppers would clutch their bags, shoot a look from hell, or walk away briskly. They might even, pre-emptively, tell the black person that they do not have any money.

So the options open to this white stranger seeking to go about puncturing privilege turn out to be an exhibition of white privilege itself. I am recalling that anecdote here because recent returns to this 'What DO black people want from me?' motif requires further examination of why this question is misdirected. Just as there is a rush to talk about 'solutions' to racism, so too is there a rush on the part of white liberals to be given a list of things to do which can release them from the bonds of unearned privilege. This request is deeply problematic.

The first problem with the question is that it instantly places a burden on me, the victim of anti-black racism, to provide whites with solutions to a historic problem in which we are *both* implicated. You, the white liberal, are outsourcing your role in the relationships that racism has generated to the people you are in a relationship *with*. You are, in effect, trying very hard, however innocent or admirable your motive, to shift the focus from yourself to the black person you are engaging. And that is, frankly, lazy. And the nature of the laziness at play here deserves exploring.

If someone who discriminated against a foreign national at their workplace is suddenly overcome with a sense of self-disappointment, it would not be praiseworthy if they sought out the victim of their xenophobia and pleaded, 'What DO you want from me? I want to help. TELL ME HOW, PLEASE!'

Of course one difference between this case and that of white liberals generally, one might argue, is that the xenophobia example is a case in which someone is *directly* responsible, and blameworthy, for the xenophobic incident to which their guilt is now oriented. But perhaps a 20-year-old, by contrast, who isn't directly responsible for colonialism or apartheid, but simply aware of their unearned privileges, should be commended for sincerely wanting to be a partner in the search for a more just society, a more comfortable space in which we all can live.

I am only partly convinced. I am in part convinced that any citizen who wishes to live in a society that is healthier than ours must be affirmed, heard, engaged and befriended. But it is only a partial agreement with the sentiment that a sincere desire to help deserves gentle or even generous engagement.

Take the sustained case study of misogyny that runs throughout this essay collection. I am not directly responsible for the acts of a particular man, or tens of thousands of men, who rape women. In that sense, the 20-year-old white man who is not directly responsible for apartheid is in a similar situation as 36-year-old me who is not directly responsible for misogyny. And, to that extent, neither of us are like the guy who was being xenophobic this morning.

But imagine I randomly called a woman, let's say a well-known feminist, and pleaded with her: 'Professor Shireen Hassim, I want to make a difference. I want to help. WHAT CAN I DO?! WHAT MUST I DO? I struck up a conversation with a woman here at the mall just now, and am taking out the film *What Women Want* to learn more. What else must I do, professor?'

I would hope that Shireen would burst out laughing, thank me for the call, and tell me to work on my anxiety on my own or with other 'progressive' men. Of course, Shireen might be generous, and actually have a conversation with me, just as I ended up chatting to the white stranger who had randomly called me a few years ago. But I honestly cannot say with certainty that I engaged that white stranger out of recognition that the guy deserved my attention. Looking back at that experience, I suspect I froze. I didn't want to be impolite in the company of a mentee-friend of mine who was witnessing it. What's clear to me is that I had no duty to soothe his anxiety, and give him a list of things to do like a Catholic priest ordering a few Hail Marys and extinguishing the sins of the previous week. Similarly, no woman has a duty to help me deal with the burdensome fact that I have a penis, and other bodily and psychological bits, that rapists also have, and which they use to oppress and violate women.

If I really want to help chip away at misogyny, it all starts with me. I need to give women a break, and focus on me, in the first instance, and boys and men.

Think about why this matters. The burden of mapping my journey out of unearned male privilege should not be placed on women. Because doing so is the equivalent of telling a victim that unless and until they come up with a prescription to treat the structural and interpersonal remnants of a misogynistic society that sponsors and enables my unearned male privilege, I might simply continue enjoying that unearned privilege. That is a cheap threat. It shows I am not serious about reflecting on the ways in which misogyny benefits me, and it shows that I do not have a strong enough desire to dismantle misogyny; if I did,

I would not lazily ask women to think for me. If I do not need women to think of the ways in which I can oppress them, or the ways in which I can benefit from their oppression, then surely I am smart enough to also figure out how to end these injustices? I am asking the wrong question of Shireen or other women if I glibly ask them to write me a prescription for my male guilt. I am not so serious about the fight against women's oppression if that is my approach.

I have a similar attitude towards homophobia. My dad, as I have narrated elsewhere, cried – bless him – when he got my letter revealing that I am gay. You would have expected him to jump for joy at the revelation that I will forever have the hormonal pleasure of skipping a heartbeat and getting a healthy erection when I see hot men. But, no, we live in a homophobic world and so Dad cried. He cried, instead of being jealous that he, sadly, was heterosexual. (No, no, don't tell me I wouldn't be here if Dad were gay. Gay men have kids too!) But here's the snag: It's simply not my role to make Dad work on his homophobia. Thank the man upstairs my dad never once said to me, 'HELP ME UNDERSTAND! WHAT MUST I DO?!'

He did have some misdirected advice for me. On one occasion, he wondered aloud if I might not want to get medical help and, on another occasion, while I was at Oxford, he wondered if I wouldn't like to have a go at dating women. I told him where to get off, and he never asked again. But in the many years during which Dad grappled with his homophobia, I can honestly say, and I salute the old timer for this, that the longest part of his journey out of homophobia was with his conscience, his own brain and in dialogue with friends and relatives who, like him, were prepared, and determined even, to 'make sense of' homosexuality on their own – and without looking up gay people in the Yellow Pages. Now, it really isn't an issue for them at all. I remain satisfied about the way I approached the matter. I am not about to dish out brownie points either for the fact that their journey out of homophobia is just about complete. Because no one should be rewarded for doing the right thing and challenging their own bigotry. That is how it should be, morally speaking. Straight people do not commend me for not being disgusted when I see them holding hands, or making love on TV and on movie screens.

The point being, of course, that I have no duty, as a gay person, to help homophobes chip away at their homophobia. I could have tried. And maybe it would have helped speed things up. But never should I be pressured into making the time. *Your bigotry, your journey.*

THE LESSON FOR WHITE LIBERALS

It is very important to understand that the request for a list of things to do to make amends for the history of colonialism and apartheid is misplaced. It is important to do other things instead, including asking the same question of *yourself*, privately, or in a dialogue with other white South Africans. That shifts the focus to working on your inner self, a self that is morally stained by the history of this strange place, and it can lead to insights about your place in this world that could be missed if you simply ask for a shopping list of actions from black friends, actions that you must perform so we can then 'move on'.

The reason this matters is partly because of the nature of racism, and the legacy of racism. Once we get a proper grip on the ways in which racism seeps through people's characters and personalities, how it manifests habitually as narcissism, and is ever-present in the minutiae of interpersonal relations, then you begin to see, from a different direction to the analysis offered here so far, why a demand for what to do is misplaced. Such a demand, if you think about it, makes it seem as if racism is *only* about what happens outside of my body, out there in the world, and that it is out there in the world where I need to go make amends, before returning to my morally untainted home, and my morally unproblematic inner self.

Well, no. Racism's reach is not restricted to the world out there. Sure, 'out there' we need material justice in terms of the nuts and bolts of how society is constructed or reconstructed. But in addition to that, as discussed elsewhere, racism requires work on the beliefs, attitudes, character traits and other psychological and social realities that enable the bad things to happen 'out there'. And that is why white liberals must do more work privately and among themselves: first, this can include a discussion of the practical question, 'What can we do out there in the world?'; but, second, it requires work on the ways in which – in how you speak, what you say, the attitudes you display – you will focus on forming new habits that show you are chipping away at your whiteness. And keep one another on your white liberal toes. Check in with a fellow white liberal to see whether an outburst on Twitter was justified, or whether it merely betrayed habituated white privilege. Don't call your black friend. *Your privilege, your journey.*

It would be really awesome to witness the effect of this work that you white liberals should do on your own, and with one another, and to notice over time the fruits of your labour, and to know I wasn't burdened with your journey, just as it was beautiful for me to watch my dad's homophobia slowly fall off him without me having to take time out from snogging men to help him out. *His bigotry, his journey.*

It's fascinating how this recommendation makes many white people uncomfortable. Or how many run for the hills. The organiser of a literary festival asked me earlier this year whether or not I wanted to be part of a panel discussion about race relations. I sighed when I got the request. It was one of my favourite literary festivals and I hope that for many years to come it will be an event I might attend annually. But the reason I sighed was because I am fatigued by the need to have an obligatory session on race relations at every local book festival and, invariably, the pressure being placed on black writers and thinkers to come and puzzle through issues of race for mostly white audiences desperate for redemption from racial anxiety. The issues relating to race do matter, for sure. But it fascinates me that there is a desire to load these panels with black people, even when over ninety per cent of authors and speakers at these events are white, as is the case with the audiences.

A few other things fascinate me about these invitations to speak on race. The first is the continued politicisation of the black body. Why not, for one festival, invite only the black participants to talk about the banality of everyday life, magical realism, the role of the essayist in society, writing for children, how romance features in modern fiction, and all sorts of other topics that speak to the complexity of a black life no less than the recognition of the diversity of interests and identity that white writers and thinkers are afforded? The very fact of these predictable themes reserved for black writers speaks to the white need to be given a shopping list of actions that they must perform to usher in a post-racial nirvana. The hope is that black writers can come and answer the question, 'What DO black people want from me?!' *Your anxiety, your journey.*

Related to this is the inability or unwillingness of white writers, thinkers and audiences to withdraw into themselves for just a moment and to explore these questions without the mediating presence of black bodies. If they were willing to 'grapple' on their own, that would show a much more genuine desire to answer the question, 'What DO black people want from me?!' And so I suggested, playfully but sincerely, that the organiser should go ahead and host a session on race relations – but, how about this: have a panel discussion that features white writers only, and a self-reflexive theme along the lines of, 'Do we moan too much about our place in this strange society of ours?' Or something along those lines – a theme that provokes deep debate, disagreement, reflection and soul searching about whiteness *among white people themselves.*

I would happily pay to attend such a session, to sit quietly at the back, and for once see white bodies in literary action grappling with race relations without burdening black writers by asking them to carry the bulk of the dialogical weight of these issues; as if black writers have special insight into racism. Since racism requires two to tango, we are all, black and white, experts on racism. So surely black writers aren't compulsory additions to panels that grapple with the place of whites in South Africa?

Or so I would have thought. The organiser, whose passion for making sense of her place in this world is matched only by her appreciation of the value of books and reading, agreed with me. And so she tried to put such a panel together. She did not succeed. Now isn't that interesting? You have, I don't know, over fifty, if not over a hundred, white writers and speakers coming to the festival already, the vast majority progressive or self-identifying as liberal, and certainly thinking of themselves as socially and politically conscious artists and writers, yet such a panel could not be put together. I don't know, to be fair, how many of these folks she emailed or called, but the organiser's commitment to put the panel together (I know from many other discussions with her leading up to the festival) would have been genuine. She would have, at the very least, put in the same effort as she had in putting together the hundred other events at the festival.

This suggests that it takes much more effort to get white writers to be on an exclusively white panel talking about whiteness than it is to get white writers to be on an exclusively white panel talking about sex scenes in works of fiction. That, I think, is neither random nor unremarkable. It is yet another exhibition of the lazy outsourcing of difficult questions about race relations to the victims of racism. It is also an attempt to avoid the emotional awkwardness of not having black bodies on stage when talking about racism; because you can lie to yourself about the prospects of dealing with the legacy of racism if the interlocutors are black and white, laughing with one another and engaging convivially. A whites-only panel would be a naked performance of the ubiquitous presence of whiteness. And not enough white South African writers are ready for that kind of visual honesty.

And that is ultimately why the question, 'What DO blacks want from me?' is a gigantic disappointment when it is posed. Not because it is posed insincerely. But because the question is an immediate revelation that even white liberals do not do the necessary private work to be taken seriously as partners in the fight against racism's legacy. White liberals must show a willingness to journey out of the heart of racism without my navigation.

Your whiteness, your journey!

CODA: REGARD FOR THE OTHER

I argued elsewhere that the impact of racism includes the ways in which racism has seeped into our attitudes, and not just racist ways in which we observably act in the public space. An attitude I have towards someone tells me how I regard that person, how they feature in my mental life.

An intimate regard for my lover or a best friend or a family member, for example, can manifest itself, in part, as a bunch of positive attitudes and other affective states: empathy; love; concern; etc. I have a positive orientation towards them, and their needs and desires and well-being matter to me. I do not merely calculate coldly about what 'they want from me'. I am so in the habit of regarding them as valuable that the question – 'What do they want from me?' – doesn't even need to be posed in such crude, awkward terms.

Now, I am not saying that whites and blacks must love each other as they do their loved ones or best friends or family members – although that is an interesting proposition worth considering on its own in a reflection on the conditions for authentic friendship, as writer Sisonke Msimang explored in her 2015 Ruth First Fellowship address. There is, nonetheless, a diagnostic truth here: part of what is grating about the question, 'What do blacks want from me?!' is that the question reveals the impoverished state of the relationship between the white liberal and her fellow black citizens. There is no proper regard for a fellow citizen. Instead, the question shows us a desire to treat 'the other' as a means to a quick end; that end being the self-satisfaction of performing a couple of actions that make awkward racial justice conversations disappear once and for all. It is a request for absolution from intergenerational racial sins, and not much more than that.

That kind of approach to race relations will never result in meaningful interracial relationships because it shows a refusal to dig deep, forge genuine friendships, and to have proper regard for the concerns and interests of anti-black racism's victims.

ARE LIBERALS INCAPABLE OF BIGOTRY?

IS UNCONSCIOUS ENJOYMENT OF
UNEARNED RACIAL PRIVILEGES PART OF
A SPECTRUM OF RACISM?

CAN I USE MY PRAISEWORTHY PAST TO STOP
FUTURE ACCUSATIONS OF RACISM?

IF MAX DU PREEZ TELLS STEVE HOFMEYR TO FUCK OFF AND DIE, DOES THAT MEAN THAT MAX CAN'T EVER BE A RACIST?

Some people convince themselves that they could not ever be racist because they have receipts that show they condemned racism in the past. The most interesting examples are white liberals, Afrikaans and English, who are embarrassed by the likes of Steve Hofmeyr, Dan Roodt, Sunette Bridges, David Bullard and other 'real' racists who routinely defend the unearned privileges of whiteness.

Yet, many white liberals who believe they have nothing in common with Roodt or Hofmeyr often display elements of racism and white privilege. Roodt, Hofmeyr and their braai buddies are not the only racists in town. They are just the loudest and the clumsiest of the lot. If they were the only purveyors of racism, then an essay collection like the one you're currently reading would not be necessary. Many white liberals, who fancy themselves to be a different species to Roodt and crew, need to be made aware of their own racism, which may not announce itself as boldly and bluntly as the most violent kinds of racism, but is there nevertheless.

Key to understanding this reality is to see racism on a spectrum: at one end you will find the most brutal physical attacks motivated by racism, and at the other end you will have a cluster of manifestations of racism and white privilege that seem innocent but which should properly be called out as part of racism's spectrum. It is at this 'innocent' end of the racism spectrum that you will find many of your favourite white liberals bunched together, throwing stompies at Hofmeyr and Roodt at the other end of the spectrum. Yet they all occupy the racism spectrum despite not liking one another.

We often distinguish 'white privilege' from 'racism'. We tend to preserve 'racism' for intentional behaviour. If someone deliberately and arbitrarily discriminates against someone else, racially, then we think they are guilty of racism. But in the expanded account of racism I argued for elsewhere in this anthology, racism also seeps into our characters, and our behaviour might display vicious ill will towards other race groups even if it is not deliberate action in the same category as wilfully getting up from your chair, walking over to someone and giving them a *klap* just because you hate their skin colour.

If racism affects us on the inside – our entire being – then we are very naïve to think that racism is a term that should only be reserved for intentional actions. We can show off a rotten 'inner self' in many ways: thinking twice about shaking someone's hand because you are 'squeamish' about shaking the hands of people of a certain skin colour; clutching your bag more tightly as you walk past men of a certain skin colour; assuming that someone who is about to address a gathering you are at will disappoint you because of what they look like; not ever being prepared to share living space with someone from another race group or even live in the same neighbourhood as them; assuming you have the vocabulary and insights to always speak for and on behalf of people of other race groups; etc.

The vicious ill will that an outright racist like Steve Hofmeyr routinely shows off is a vicious ill will that can also be present in white critics of Steve Hofmeyr, once we accept that a spectrum of behaviour can flow from the kind of viciousness that lurks in a racist's heart.

This is not to imply that every white person is necessarily racist. That would be evidently false. But every white person benefits or has benefited from unearned white privilege just as every male benefits from ever-present misogyny. The consequence of unchosen benefits is that how you respond to that fact determines whether or not you are on the continuum of racism/sexism. Living completely obliviously to these unearned privileges, and assuming, for example, that only your individual efforts explain your life achievements, places you on the non-bloody end of the racism/sexism spectrum. You belong there, deserve criticism, and are not yet in an appropriate, genuine relationship with the victims of racism/sexism. You can be taken off the racism/sexism spectrum, not by only avoiding overt public acts of bigotry, but by actively eliminating your unearned privileges and guarding against unintended displays of white/male supremacist ideologies. This requires recognition of the ways in which your white skin privileges you purely on account of your being white – like the fact that your competency is not routinely doubted because of your skin colour – and it requires actively working to reduce the material inequities around you that have come about because of the long history of white supremacy and anti-black racism, and colonialism. You cannot, for example, be opposed to redistributive policies designed to democratise the economy, and opportunities to create wealth among black people, yet self-identify as someone committed to end racism. We can quibble about particular policies' effectiveness, but you must be on board with racial redress as a fundamental requirement of a more just South Africa if I'm going to take you seriously as a white ally in the fight against racism.

So it is hard and takes work not to be on the racism spectrum at all. And it should be unsurprising then that even white critics of violent white racists are themselves not immune to the vestiges of racism and unearned privilege.

MAX DU PREEZ: THE LIE ABOUT VIRTUOUS LIBERALS

At the beginning of 2015, *Rapport* carried an interview with writer Max du Preez. The interviewer asked Du Preez at some stage what he would like to say to Hofmeyr and Bridges. His response? 'Fuck off and die.'[6] He continued, 'They are the enemies of Afrikaners, and white people. They – and Roodt – have done more damage to the lot of Afrikaans people than anyone else over the past 100 years.'

Park these remarks for a second. The interview continued with Du Preez going on, not only about these embarrassing Afrikaners, but at the same time critiquing the current African National Congress-led government, and the state in general. This is where things got really interesting. How I wish the interview had been carried in an English paper, so that a wider readership could see Du Preez for who he really is.

He went on to say that Zelda la Grange, Nelson Mandela's former assistant (who had the audacity to go on Twitter and try to imply that whites are under siege in South Africa) was 'misunderstood' and that she should not be bothered by criticism of her on social media platforms. What she wanted to say was legitimate, but unlike him, she wasn't a 'sophisticated political activist'. Just as well I didn't have a mug of coffee in my hand, since I would almost certainly have dropped it in disbelief. Is this the Du Preez every liberal and their mother tried to write poetic defences of in early 2015 as the ANC needlessly attacked him for an opinion piece about President Zuma, a defence which involved some people, rather dramatically, even posting

---

6 http://www.netwerk24.com/stemme/2015-01-25-hanlie-retief-gesels-met-max-du-preez

pictures with the caption, 'Je Suis Max du Preez', implying he was a victim of terrorist proportions? But, brace yourself, more was to come.

Du Preez then tried to correct the La Grange 'misunderstanding' by lecturing black South Africans in his own words: 'Black South Africans still haven't wrapped their heads around the fact that you (the interviewer) and I are not colonialists, that our forebears were, but that it is now 400 years later ... My forebears are not me. I was not at Vlakplaas. I did not shoot the Khoi at Riebeek Valley. My forebears did. That is not my fault. Because I am a good South African citizen, I have the right to say it was them, my forebears. I take responsibility but it is not my fault.'

And then Du Preez left us with a paternalistic, final, Bullard-esque thrust: 'We must, in a nice way, say to black South Africans: *Deal with it*. Why is South Africa different to the rest of Africa? Why can *we* host a World Cup Soccer-tournament? When our ancestors came here, they did terrible things, but they also brought other things with them, and that is the mix that is now here. Blacks can't do without us, and we can't do without them ... '

THE PAST ISN'T IMMUNITY FROM FUTURE WRONGDOING

There is a lot here that is fascinating. Du Preez was deeply insulted, as were his fans, by the accusation from the presidency and many in the ANC, that he could be a racist. When he ended his relationship with Independent Media as a columnist, he prefaced that decision with a long summary of his work as a journalist during the repressive days of apartheid. He reminded the world, essentially in an open letter (it was, ahem, 'leaked'), that he has amazing struggle-media credentials, including as editor of *Vrye Weekblad*. It was, by unsubtle implication, an insult to even dare imagine him capable of racism.

Many outright white racists consider Du Preez to be crawling up the asses of black people. SO, how could Du Preez possibly be a racist given his struggle credentials as well as the opprobrium meted out to him by his own? Add to that the fact that he told Hofmeyr and Bridges to 'fuck off and die', and you surely have someone who is the exemplar of white progressive thought and politics. Surely? Not quite.

It is important to scrutinise the lies here about white liberals. Du Preez is a useful case study precisely because for many he is an *uncontested* example of white progressive thought.

First, it is mind-boggling to me that someone can regard their past as proof of future innocence. Hypothetically, if I give you an example of this one time when I was 18 and I beat up a bunch of guys that tried to assault a woman, would that make me immune to any future sexism or unearned male privileges?

Of course not. We can expand this example. Let's say I didn't just come to a woman's rescue once, but had a good reputation for being in the *habit* of pointing out sexism, calling out men who engage in sexist behaviour, and standing up for women who are victims of such bigotry. Would such a reputation mean I am incapable of violating a woman myself, maltreating female colleagues at the office, or abusing my wife? Of course not. My capacity for evil is not wiped out by a few praiseworthy actions. My capacity for wrongdoing is enduring. It is a feature of my humanity.

Du Preez wants a free pass from racism's reach. Merely having worked at *Vrye Weekblad* does not mean you are incapable of racism. The capacity for racism, like the capacity for sexism, follows us everywhere. Even Mandela was capable of racism and sexism. So white liberals need to rid themselves of the belief that they are inherently incapable of racism. They are not. Just as I am not immune to exhibiting racism on account of being black. I am not even immune to homophobia just on account of being gay. We must quit these demands to be treated as perfectly virtuous. That is a pipe dream.

DU PREEZ'S SOFT BIGOTRY

I had a horrible experience in 2014 at a pub in Melville. A flamboyant, gay white owner by the name of J – and don't worry, I will explain the relevance of this depiction in a second – who knew me well had the gall to exhibit his racism in front of me.

After I asked him whether he too had been raided, like other restaurants and pubs on 7th Street that night, he told me that black cops had come in demanding some payment for the musical entertainment, which was not part of his licensing conditions. He followed this up by telling me something along the lines of, 'I know, Eusebius, that some of us love black cock, but really ... these bloody *kaffirs*!'

My two friends and I left a few minutes later. I have not been back there since, and the vile racist can't make eye contact with me when he sees me because I documented the story in one of my newspaper columns thereafter. The reason I mention that he is gay, and flamboyant, is that – and I certainly own this stereotype about to follow – many of us assume that if someone knows what it is like to be a minority or if they know what it is like to be the victim of arbitrary discrimination, they will be less likely to be a bigot than others who have no such experience to draw on. Effeminate men, gay or straight, often suffer verbal, physical and emotional abuse from gender police who think that male bodies must be butch. I had to endure this kind of verbal abuse in primary school because I was effeminate.

And so many of us think that white gay men are probably less likely to be racist than heterosexual white men. But this is a myth that is routinely shattered when I interact with many white gay men, and women. Racism runs deep, and does not discriminate between sexual orientations. As the bar owner teaches us.

The difference between J and Steve Hofmeyr is that, for most of the time, the racism is soft. It doesn't manifest itself in the same overt way as the racism of someone who beats people up because of their skin colour. The use of the word *kaffir*, I am sure, was a rare slip for him. You would have to sit at his bar and observe his interaction with his young black staff very closely to see how soft, but clear the abuse of power – a toxic combination of racist supremacist attitudes and economic power – really is. Or speak off the record to some who have worked there, as I have done.

And this is where we return to Du Preez. If we closely examine the excerpts from the interview in *Rapport*, the remnants of racial supremacy are clear, and as morally problematic as the less controversial exemplars of racism.

It's interesting that Du Preez describes Hofmeyr and Roodt as enemies of Afrikaners. He doesn't declare them *in the first instance* enemies of black people or, as you would expect from a colour-blind progressive white person, enemies of all decent South Africans. Why would Du Preez put it this way? I shall hazard a guess. Because, clearly, it is the bad reputation that Afrikaners might get as a result of what Hofmeyr and Roodt say that most irks Du Preez. If that was not his biggest gripe, why start off a critique of them by prioritising the effect of their racism on the place and reputation of the Afrikaner community (as opposed to the effect of their racism on racism's victims)?

This is astounding if you consider the self-ascribed history of fighting racism with his pen that Du Preez brags about in his open letter, explaining why he is quitting a column in a newspaper he no longer deems credible. Well, if it is the battle against anti-black racism that most defines your past writing, then surely what should first and foremost piss you off royally about Roodt and Hofmeyr must be their racism, and the meaning of that racism for black people, not for white people who are beyond the reach of the racist's poisonous spit?!

I expected the white liberal to articulate, with Albie Sachs-like lyricism, what the content of the views of Roodt and Hofmeyr do to the dignity of black people. But that is not Du Preez's central concern here. He is speaking Afrikaans, to Afrikaners, and he is asking them to be prudent about their community's reputation in wider South Africa by not supporting Roodt or Bridges or Hofmeyr. Doesn't that sound less like a principled opposition to naked racism than a strategy session for how best to locate yourself in the country-at-large? So much for the moral virtues of being a moderate or a progressive or a liberal or whatever the preferred label for whites who say to Hofmeyr, 'Fuck off and die'.

I consider this an instance of the soft bigotry of racism. It is bigoted to be so self-indulgent about 'your people' that your chief problem with a racist in your midst is that they are bad for 'your people'. A genuine commitment to rooting out racism requires you to focus on and condemn the intrinsic moral evil of the racism itself. You should get 'your people' to see racism for what it is, not incentivise them to keep the tribal brand untainted, which is at best a very oblique way of exposing racism in your ranks.

This is compounded by the bizarre claim by Du Preez that Hofmeyr and Bridges have done more damage to the lot of Afrikaners than anyone else 'in the past 100 years'. Huh?! If Du Preez thinks that this is the worst reputational damage that Afrikaners have suffered since 1915, then he obviously has a very short memory. Surely the bloody violence of apartheid perpetrated by Afrikaner nationalists was even worse than the post-apartheid rhetoric of unreconstructed apartheid fossils like Bridges and Hofmeyr?

Look, I'm not saying Du Preez shouldn't be pissed off with Bridges and Hofmeyr. He should. We all should. But I am certainly suggesting that the careful reader shouldn't be hoodwinked into praising Du Preez too soon here. Because, in virtue of Du Preez casually regarding these contemporary racists as the worst of its Afrikaner kind in the past 100 years, he shows the luxury of not being burdened, daily, by the personal memory of the worst acts of violence against blacks. In fact, you trivialise that memory of anti-black racism if you think that a few choice quotes from Hofmeyr are the most embarrassment a progressive Afrikaner can feel these days.

I am not surprised though: whites need only ever worry about saving face in the moment. Blacks, however, have history thrust upon us in the present. We can't neatly enjoy life in democratic South Africa with a linear conception of time. Our conception of time is more discombobulated than Du Preez's because the past remains our reality. Du Preez, by contrast, shares an ahistorical attitude with Hofmeyr – the past ended in 1994 and only post-94 embarrassments matter for Du Preez – while imagining himself, in rebuking Hofmeyr, to be distancing himself from Hofmeyr. But that self-congratulatory rebuke, upon careful scrutiny, is less applause-worthy than you might think at first. White privilege really is nice, isn't it?

The excerpt from Du Preez also highlights an 'us versus them' distinction that runs throughout his remarks with gay abandon. There is the constant reference to 'black South Africans' as a homogenous group, and even though he refers to Afrikaners too as a community, at least they are allowed to be less homogenous, with a distinction implicit in his remarks between racist Afrikaners and non-racist Afrikaners. So at the very least there are two different kinds of Afrikaners. But all blacks, of course, have an essence that all blacks share, and hence Du Preez tells the interviewer how 'black South Africans' think all whites are colonialists. There is no distinction here between black people, just a very comfortable generalisation. Quite apart from the generalisation being false – I have yet to meet a black person who regards *all* whites as colonialists – it is the comfort with which blacks are referred to here as a homogenous group that truly irks.

In *A Bantu in my Bathroom* I argued that racial categories are not inherently immoral. This is what I referred to there as racialism. It is what you do with the categories that determine whether or not you are being racist. If you use racial categories to discriminate arbitrarily between race groups, then you are committing racism, which is morally indefensible. So racialism, in my analysis, can be innocuous, and the real enemy of a just society is racism. Group identities are not necessarily a problem. Racism is. The two things are not the same.

I say this because I want to be clear that I do 'see' race. Colour-blindness is impossible for any South African born here, and who lives here. So, like Du Preez, I too make a distinction between blacks and whites. I am not trying to skewer Du Preez merely because he divides the world into race groups.

The reason I mock Du Preez for his racial distinctions in the context of the remarks he made in the *Rapport* interview is because of the hypocrisy in our public debate about this racialism. Du Preez, like many South Africans, is routinely repulsed by any explicit reference to racial categories in public policy language, in the blogosphere, on social media platforms, in a collection of essays like this one, on talk radio platforms, and around *chisa nyamas*. Yet when *they* use racial categories, the rest of us are expected to hear or read this racial indexing differently from how we are heard or read when we reference blacks or whites or any racial description we might use on a particular occasion.

The thinking is that there is something amoral and intellectually considered about the use of racial labels by someone like Du Preez; in other words, they don't really mean to use racial categories willy-nilly but do so, grudgingly, and instrumentally, in the service of establishing some grand insight. That is the kind of conversational courtesy we are expected to grant self-professed white progressives.

Well, I refuse to do so because racialism is knowledge in our South African blood. No one performs racialism as a thought experiment. Neither Hofmeyr nor Du Preez. Their utterances are variations on the same racial self-identity; they are not different species even if Du Preez thinks it is cool to swear at Hofmeyr in the biggest Afrikaans newspaper. Sorry, Max, but that was a party trick, *boet*.

WHEN DU PREEZ CHANNELS DAVID BULLARD

I earlier described a quote from Du Preez as Bullard-inspired. To paraphrase that quote, Du Preez intimated that black people should be grateful for all the positive contributions Du Preez's ancestors have made to the development of South Africa.

I do not see a relevant difference between this statement and the column that rightly received a backlash from the public and got Bullard fired for racism and bigotry. Bullard, we dare not forget, in a very unfunny column, basically thought about what might have happened if we natives had never been colonised. He imagined an alternative, colonialism-free Africa to be a place that remains hugely undeveloped with blacks basically bonking to keep themselves busy, having kids left, right and centre, presumably out of undeveloped animal instinct untouched by the beauty of colonial values. Ever since being sacked for that column, he has clamoured for relevance by being a social media troll, initiating countless fake legal cases to try to defend an imagined good reputation. No doubt he will smile at the anecdotal inclusion of his racism in this essay, also because the racist troll's need is simple: he just wants his existence to be acknowledged.

But this comparison is less about Bullard (sorry Mr Bullard) and in fact about the liberal white South African who thinks that sharing a sense of disgust at the naked racism of Bullard buys them, in turn, the right not to be scrutinised or called out on their unconscious bathing in whiteness. And that is why this interview with Du Preez was so indicative of a trap that anyone committed to fighting anti-black racism shouldn't fall for, that is, that weird feeling that you're being condescended to because you are seen as incapable of excellence in the absence of white colonisers – *but for us arriving here this place would be underdeveloped!* – yet you feel you could not possibly call out Du Preez because he too hates Hofmeyr!

Well, let's cut to the central claim of this essay: it is a false dichotomy to think that a white person is either a racist of Hofmeyr proportions or they are progressive. There are, I am afraid, degrees of racism, degrees of whiteness, degrees of privilege. Max du Preez and David Bullard are not fundamentally different kinds of moral beings in our racism-drenched society. They are simply variations on a theme. You can choose, as with Oros, how you like racism served to you in this country: weak or strong. But you cannot deny the taste of a famous brand, be it Oros or Good Old Racism. Du Preez and Bullard have more in common than either would admit.

WHAT BEST EXPLAINS THE DISPROPORTIONATE
WEALTH AND ACHIEVEMENTS OF WHITES?

IS 'MERITOCRACY' AN OBJECTIVE CONCEPT?

DOES ECONOMIC JUSTICE REQUIRE 'LOWERING
THE BAR' FOR WOMEN AND BLACK PEOPLE?

MERITOCRACY, WHITE EXCELLENCE AND OTHER MYTHS

I got a call a few weeks ago from a world-class expert on organisational culture. She had been doing a fascinating piece of research for a regular corporate client. The company wanted her to find out what the experiences of women and black people are inside the firm. Using robust methodologies, she proceeded to do precisely that and was now ready to share the results with the top leadership of the company. So why call me, I wondered?

The researcher – call her Kate – wanted me to help her communicate her research findings and recommendations to the client. She felt that, with my understanding of philosophy and communication, I might ably assist her in articulating a narrative the leadership needed to understand if this company was to go from very good to great, and perhaps even become a leader on how to be, as she described it from language used in her discipline, 'culturally agile'. Because of my interest in questions of identity, I immediately said yes, and met Kate to get a full grasp of what the research questions were, how she had gone about the research, what she had found and what her recommendations were. It was fascinating, to put it mildly.

The results of the research were not surprising at all. In fact, she could have been talking about any company or institution in our country. Let me describe some of the findings, and I have no doubt that most readers – certainly black people and women – will agree that these findings could have been a depiction of the company they – you – work for in this troubled country of ours.

Kate found a number of dominant themes in the stories from her interviews, which included interviews with lower-tier employees, managers and leaders in various parts of the company. One that consistently surfaced was that the company was already doing its bit for the country and ought not to be pressured by the state or other actors in society to do more. The company employs over 8 000 workers, contributes positively to the economic growth figures of our country, and the products and services offered by this company help tens of thousands of South Africans to live flourishing lives. It was, so this narrative goes, a great South African brand that could be proud of its place under the new South African sun.

A second narrative that came through strongly was that there was a trade-off between merit and transformation. Many managers and leaders of the company felt strongly that inherent in the idea of 'transformation' was a lowering of standards for the instrumental purpose of allowing more women and black staff into the company and up the corporate ladder without simply letting them be measured against the objective standards of a meritocracy, which was what this company had always been. The view was that one could not be both a meritocracy and a place that adopts transformation policies.

An interesting third dominant narrative, specifically from black and female staff who were interviewed, was that there was insufficient transparency in the publication of criteria used to promote some people but not others. In addition to and related to this lack of transparency, one needed to have a sponsor in the leadership structure to facilitate and champion your career inside the company. Without someone batting for you when discussions about promotions happened, regardless of your actual performance on the job, you would be disadvantaged in the race to the top. Yet, accessing the social networks that, in turn, enabled these relationships between leaders and other employees, proved tough for most women and most black people. The feeling was that this inaccessibility to the networks was worsened by a failure on the part of the leaders of the company to see the role that networking plays in one's career trajectory.

Finally, a small group of interviewees were simply indifferent about the entire research subject, not convinced that it would make an iota of difference, and that it was the kind of research that way too many companies waste money on, instead of getting on with useful economic activity.

Isn't that an amazing set of findings, on the one hand, and yet, on the other, completely unsurprising if you live consciously in a South Africa structured by legacies of colonialism, apartheid, and misogyny? What was interesting was how the findings of Kate, who is a phenomenally insightful and internationally experienced author, consultant and lecturer in this field, were rejected by many of the top leaders once we proceeded to present her findings.

Very perceptively, when Kate pulled all her research findings together, and drilled down into some of the other quantitative data about the experiences of black and female staff (e.g. Who gets hired? What kinds of projects and responsibilities are they assigned? How long do they stay in the company? etc.), an important overarching conclusion jumped out at her. It became clear to her that the gap between the uncritical pride of most of the top leadership about their company being a South African rock star, and the troubling, varied experiences of female and black staff, is explained by the myth of meritocracy.

Kate did not have the philosophical tools at her disposal that I do, and so we divided the presentation accordingly. My role was to critically interrogate the notion of meritocracy, which lay at the heart of the insistence by a majority of the members of the board that the organisational culture was friendly to women and black people. Kate, in turn, was to present the specific details of what had come out of her research, and what this meant for the company going forward.

I felt emotionally drained after spending over an hour with

the leadership. It was, of course, a board dominated by white men. One white woman spoke frequently, pushing back against the resistance to Kate's evidence-based results. And the black woman who owned the transformation portfolio showed mettle in insisting that the white men disrupt Kate less frequently, and actually listen to the reported experiences of people fundamentally different from them. But the Group CEO was a real gem, and his buy-in meant that this company would stay with this conversation, and implement the findings. But, in general, the uncritical belief in a perfect meritocracy shone through in the scepticism of many of the questions, interventions and disagreements.

If I were not a trained debater and public speaker, and confident of my views on race, gender, and transformation in the context of racism's legacy, I may have buckled under the pressure. But, as always, I said it as I see it, and to the leadership's credit, they allowed for a space of mutual respect.

So, what does all this have to do with racism, you may wonder? If you do not interrogate why some groups are over-represented in some sectors of society then you will miss the embedded racism in our social structures that keep some out and others in. You will also, I'm afraid, swallow the lie, if you're a beneficiary of racism's legacy, that nothing other than good genes and sheer hard work explain why you, a white man, ended up being the CEO of your company and a poor black guy born the same day as you at a state hospital, is your gardener. The truth, I'm afraid, is that in South Africa it is mythical to imagine that the history of colonialism and racism cannot possibly be part of the explanation of 'white excellence'.

I made this point to the company's leadership by drawing on my experiences in competitive debate, and my observations about how women are treated in competitive debate. It is instructive to share that experience, because it illuminates the myth of meritocracies elsewhere, before we return to the myth of white excellence in corporate South Africa.

COMPETITIVE DEBATE AND GENDER BIAS

Kate presented first. She knows the client well and she is brilliant at her work. She is soft-spoken and has a quiet presence. She is small in stature and does not project her voice much. At the presentation, she was polite and discursive, and even when challenged she replayed the comment of the interjector to affirm him and to give some weight to his intuitions, before responding. Her comportment was feminine, one might say, and her body language, including the space she occupied, closed and small. Her content was her greatest source of authority.

There are many downsides to being a competitive, trained debater. But the downsides, in the context of this discussion, are irrelevant. The plus sides of being trained are illuminating in what played out next. When I addressed the leadership of this company after Kate, I think it is fair to say, the energy levels increased. I have a bigger physical presence and a loud, booming voice. I wore a power suit matching any of those in the room but with a screaming pink tie to assert my individuality. My body language was open and I took up as much leg and other bodily space as I wished. I spoke without written notes, having memorised the key concepts I wanted to explore, and this freed me up to look every person in the eye during my allotted time.

I spoke fluently, with clear structure and signposting and when the men tried their disrupting tactics, I matched their masculinity by telling the person concerned to hold his horses until I had completed a thought or an analogy before I gave him permission to offer a point of information.

I also spoke directly about competitive debate and public speaking. 'Most of you probably find me more compelling than you did Kate, as a speaker.' I asserted that with typical male arrogance but feeling self-assured that most, if not all of them, secretly agreed.

'I am, to be fair, trained in debating, and have won the National South African Universities Debate Championships, as well as the World Master's Debate Championships.'

At this point, one of the more overzealous sceptics interrupted me, someone who had earlier accused Kate of misreading her data, and had argued that the experiences of black people and women apply to every person, including white men, trying to succeed in any company. As I was listing the debating competitions I had won as a student, he quipped, 'Did you win them on merit?' Everyone laughed. It was, yeah, a decent joke, and a nice little puncturing of a potentially awkward atmosphere given that these conversations are deeply personal and never merely about 'the company'. I chuckled too. He had played directly into my strategy. And my response caught him off guard.

'Actually, funny you should ask that. No, I won partly because I have a penis!' Some awkward chuckles were forthcoming and puzzled looks stared back at me. 'That's precisely why I want to talk about competitive debate and public speaking as a useful activity through which to unravel the myths of meritocracy. Sure, I worked hard at debate, and in many ways deserve some of the wins of my career. But having a penis, an accident of birth I did not choose, helped me enormously!'

In debating, you get points allocated for the strength of your argument, your strategic decisions about what arguments to elect and how to respond to your competitors, and points for your manner or style of speaking. But, technicalities aside, and different debate formats aside, the basic question an adjudicator asks when determining who wins a debate is, 'Who was most persuasive?' Persuasiveness is a function, on paper at least, of content, strategy and persuasive style or manner.

More men than women win the competitions that I won. I have been involved in competitive debate at tertiary level since 1997 and remained actively involved for over ten years. During that time I noticed that women still struggled to win tournaments even as the number and percentage of women participating in debating increased. It is not, like soccer or golf or netball, a competitive activity where male dominance can be explained by the disproportionate non-participation of one of the sexes. So, if men dominate the speaker ranking at debate tournaments, and more male debate teams win competitions than female debate teams, why might that be?

The reason has to do with my sex. We have to accept that a loud voice, projection, the confidence to hold up your hand to halt an interjector, asserting that an interlocutor is wrong, are markers of greater communicative skill. It is not obvious that Kate is less compelling than me. After all, she is the expert, and not me. And she did the research on the company, not me. And she has the material they can use to go from good to great, not me. So how is it that my intervention can seem equally or more important? Because traits that are more prevalent in male bodies are uncritically assumed to be markers of confidence, and persuasiveness. If someone is not loud and does not accentuate every phrase for dramatic effect, but speaks a little more slowly, softly and their voice doesn't fill the room easily, they are dismissed as unpersuasive. But a huge dose of testosterone in a public speaker, performing at the podium with macho certainty like a rugby fan winning a debate about who should be selected as a Springbok with his mates at the pub … that makes you a good debater, a good speaker.

A few feminine women have excelled at debating. But they are exceptions. Most of the very small number of women who excel at competitive debate end up mimicking the behaviour of male speakers; they are loud, even boisterous, aggressive in tone, always certain of the a priori truths coming out their mouths, and even use intimidating tactics like barracking or, while an opponent offers you a point of information, walking right up to them while they speak in an attempt to undermine their confidence in what they are asking.

Nothing in the past few paragraphs makes reference to brilliant content, thoughtful argument and analytic skill. So, to be fair on the countless men in debate who are brilliant, I want to make it clear that part of why many of the champion male debaters are champions is because most of them think long and hard about moral, political and economic issues, read widely, can reason analytically, have a good intuitive grasp of logic or are trained in formal and informal logic, and are genuinely good speakers. Also, not all of them are aggressive, and many are funny, and quiet.

But that is, in a sense, the deeper point here. Precisely because so many men in debating genuinely have good genes, and genuinely work hard to win tournaments, it is easy to think that genes plus effort are the sum total of the reasons they excel. If I put in 10 000 hours to become a debate expert, I would be mortally upset if a woman came along and said that my penis is an important arbitrary reason why I win a lot.

But that person would have a point. It is possible, and this is reality, that good genes, plus effort, can be boosted by unearned privileges. If, for example, the history of the world played out differently, and traits more commonly associated with women were regarded as markers of persuasive speaking, then many men would struggle to win competitions even with good genes and hard work. If a deep, booming voice was associated with, say, uncertainty, and lack of faith in your words, then male speakers would have to dig deeper to be persuasive. Worse, if having a slight frame and small body and not sprawling your legs and taking up a lot of physical space were crucial to being regarded as 'having presence', then men would in fact have genetic bad luck! The truth, then, is that the history of misogyny benefits all men, including men who genuinely put in the hours, and who are gifted by Mother Nature with good genes. It is a total fabrication to think that the unchosen fact of being male doesn't give you a head start in competitive debate. It does.

And so at the presentation with Kate I ended my example by trying to challenge my own arrogant assertion that Kate was less compelling than me. I insisted that if any of the leadership in the room were thinking critically about how all men benefit from sexism, they would have to revise their impressions of Kate's public speaking ability and consider to what extent their impressions piggybacked on sexist tropes about what a good speaker looks and sounds like.

I cannot claim that the titles I have won in competitive debate tournaments are only the result of effort and genetic luck: it was that, plus the accent of masculinity that flows from me being male, and having the kinds of biological characteristics that enable masculine performances more readily than if I was female. So, in response to the quip of the executive when I showed my debate and public speaking receipts: no, my debating CV isn't purely a CV of meritorious achievement; my debating achievements were enabled, in small part (no pun intended), by the fact that I have a penis.

The extended example was well received. I think if you excel at an activity and your audience can see that you do – like public speaking – it is harder for them not to take seriously your reflections on why your 'achievement' isn't just a matter of merit. Public speaking is also less emotional a topic to discuss than race. And so the point, I think, was already understood at a general level: the language of meritocracy is deceptive in a world where arbitrary facts can intervene in the trajectory of one's career. But it was important, of course, to tie the lesson to the discourse of race and organisational culture.

RACISM'S PRESENCE IN THE CORPORATE SECTOR

Most people in senior management positions in South Africa are white and most of the wealth and assets of the country are owned by white people, including those listed on the Johannesburg Stock Exchange. Of course, this is despite the fact that white people do not even constitute ten per cent of the population of the country.

This dominance is not restricted to the distribution of wealth. It is also true of many other sectors of society. Year in, and year out, the majority of top matriculants finishing high school in South Africa are white students. And in sporting codes where you have a mix of race groups now competing with one another, like in rugby, you still have an overrepresentation of white players at national level, and in some provinces. As I noted earlier, if you check out literary festivals, you will find more white than black writers in charge of chronicling the stories and facts about life in this country, despite whites being a small minority. There surely cannot be another country in the world where a minority group this small, relative to other groups, enjoys such incredible amounts of success. It is perhaps only when it comes to party politics, really, that white South Africans are as influential as you would expect – that is, not very much. But in other spheres of South African life the opposite is true, including in the company that Kate and I were engaging.

What explains this dominance of the white minority in, for example, the corporate sector in South Africa? In the interviews that Kate had conducted, of course, it was clear that the winners in the company – those in top positions – strongly believed that effort and genes were at the heart of their career journeys. Their idea of being sensitive to women or black people was to make sure that these groups had 'equal opportunities' and then, of course, it was up to them to make the most of those opportunities.

There is incredible hubris here. If it is true that the two main explanations of white achievement are good genes and hard work, then the implication, surely, is that black underachievement is either a result of bad genes, laziness or both. That thought, if anyone dared to think or express it, is both demonstrably false and racist. It is racist because it shows a vicious ill will towards black people in respect of their capability as humans. Unless black people are of a different species, there is no reason to imagine a black child inherently less capable of being the top matriculant in the country than a white child.

Mother Nature distributes talent randomly in the human population. Intellectual capacity in particular is a matter of individual luck. Some things are more prevalent in some groups, and so we might, for example, puzzle through the dominance of Kenyan runners in long-distance events or African-Americans in basketball or Asians in maths and science, etc. But not only is this handful of examples disproportionate to the incredibly widespread dominance of white people in many aspects of South African life, but these exceptions are not always a matter of genetic luck. Sometimes environmental factors, like how you raise your children, can determine the level of competency they might have when it comes to maths and science, or training at high altitude if you're an athlete.

But this brings us closer to some home truths. If black people are not born lazy, and if black people do not have genes that are inferior to those of white people, then hard work and good genes do not complete the story of white dominance in corporate South Africa. There has to be an invisible hand at work here, or an environmental factor. Or maybe this is one and the same thing.

It's not rocket science figuring this one out. The unearned privilege of being born into a white skin in South Africa immediately gives you many advantages over a baby born into a black skin. If you are a white baby, there is less of a chance that you will be born into poverty. Related to that, there is a better chance, if you're the white baby, that you will grow up inside or into established social networks that you can leverage when you leave school. There is a far greater chance that, as a white graduate, you will not be the first person in your family to go to university, and you will likely have fewer relatives depending on your salary when you enter the job market. A black baby, statistically speaking, will grow up with fewer resources than her white counterpart, have many more 'odds' to beat to complete school, let alone to complete it with excellent results, and have to enter a job market with few if any connections and mentors to learn from, and lean on.

The history of anti-black racism, dating back to colonial times and most recently sharpened by the architects of apartheid, entrenched these unnatural advantages for the white population. Does a white baby choose to be white? Of course not. Is a white baby born today responsible for the evil of Hendrik Verwoerd? Of course not. Does it follow from all of this that a white child is not a beneficiary of racism at the expense of her black generational peers?

No. Because we can benefit against our will. That is how the world is structured. That is exactly the lesson from the competitive debate example. Did I choose to be born male and to have more testosterone than women? No. Is it my fault that I was born into a sexist world that systemically oppresses women? No. Am I a beneficiary, against my will, of the history of misogyny and its present-day manifestations? Absolutely I am!

But the point that really irks an unthinking white guy who imagines himself a hard-working person deserving of his 'meritorious' achievements is that a refusal to accept the role that luck plays in his life is racist. No really. If a white person cannot accept that luck, in the form of unearned white privilege, boosts their career trajectory and corporate achievements, then they are displaying a racist attitude. The reason is simple: to deny that luck plays some role in the story of how you came to be a wealthy corporate executive is to endorse the view that blacks are either lazy or genetically inferior to you. You can only escape this racism charge by understanding and accepting that your achievements are sponsored by the history of white supremacist systems the world over that gave you structural advantages from the day you were born.

It's the same with competitive debating. If a guy refuses to accept the systemic ways in which women are disadvantaged by the stereotypes in debate about what persuasive speaking consists of, then they are being sexist. Because implicit in this refusal to accept that being male helps your debating career is an inadvertent suggestion that female debaters are either lazy or have inferior genes.

No doubt some readers will think one can be innocently ignorant about the role of luck in one's achievements. And if a white CEO never thought about how he benefits from whiteness, and a male debater never thought critically about gender norms in debate, then accusations of racism and sexism are clumsy, if not unfair.

I disagree. I think the reason we refuse to talk about this kind of culpable ignorance as instances of racism – or sexism – is precisely because we think racism is only racism if it is bloody and crude. But non-bloody racism operates in this kind of shrewd way, as do sexist attitudes that do not leave a visible scar on a woman's body.

Where does this leave the concept of 'meritocracy'? It is not a concept that cannot be made sense of at all, but it is a term that should not be hastily used in the context of an unequal society with a history of structural injustices. In our context, the pretence that an organisation is founded on a culture of meritocracy can lead to laziness. Firstly, it can lead to the uncritical belief among the winners in that organisation that their experiences define the organisational culture. Secondly, it can lead to the uncritical belief that sheer hard work explains success. And, thirdly, most damaging perhaps, it can lead to a refusal to rethink the organisational culture and to intervene to ensure that the company or institution comes closer to being a genuine meritocracy, and not a place where white skin or male genitalia give you a head start.

CONCLUDING THOUGHTS

I genuinely sympathise with hard-working white men who put in long hours to exploit their genes in order to succeed in life. Some of my best friends and mentors are white men who work enormously hard to be brilliant writers, lawyers, businessmen, academics, etc. And if you work so hard, it must feel puzzling to be asked to consider yourself lucky.

After all, you may know other white men who were lazy who

are now unemployed or working as a cashier at a bottle store. Since you are both white, surely you deserve praise and credit for investing in yourself? It's not as though you were born with your achievements. If that were true, the white guy from your school who is now working at the bottle store should also have been born with guaranteed success. The tiebreaker, it seems from this reasoning, is hard work. Not white luck.

That, I admit, makes sense for a few seconds. But it ignores the reality that in effect you compete with a handful of individuals who are in a similar situation to you. You can't be said to fairly compete with a poor black guy in a township who is your age. So your white skin automatically means you beat some people in the human race just because of where they are structurally situated in society. Your hard work is real. But the external factors that reduce the level of competition you are facing are also real. Your hard work can be acknowledged and applauded while simultaneously being situated in the context of unearned white privileges. And that is the reason why white excellence should not be seen as just.

This doesn't mean that the ideal of a meritocracy makes no sense. The idea of an institution or society in which people are merely entitled to equal opportunities and the rest is up to them, is coherent. But when you truly understand the injustice of social structures and even biology arbitrarily determining your chances of doing well in the race, then you have reason to help work towards eliminating structural injustices.

In practice, this means being a company, for example, that

asks itself such questions as, 'Did we evaluate Kate as not ready to be partner because she lacks confidence? Or did we conclude she lacks confidence because of gender bias in our evaluation criteria for "communication excellence?"' And, when Jabu applies for a job and makes it through the tests but 'doesn't seem like he belongs' here, you may want to ask, 'Is Jabu really not one of us? Or are we reinforcing the ability to speak English like us and our kids, and talk rugby and golf, as markers of cultural fit in this organisation?'

The more conscious a company or an individual is about luck and structural injustice, the more likely it is that they will treat others fairly. That is not lowering the bar for success. That is realising that the image of a bar being lowered is one we must discard in conversations about transformation. You are asked to be aware of unconscious bias rather than being asked to drop standards for women or black people. In the country we currently live, there are still enormous amounts of unfairness. And blacks and women are the biggest losers. The beneficiaries of racism sleep easily by lying to themselves. They go to bed thinking that sheer hard work explains why they are better off than most of the country. That's a comforting lie.

IS THERE PLACE FOR EMOTION IN DIALOGUE?

DOES ANGER HAVE ANY MORAL OR
PRACTICAL VALUE?

CAN THE EXPRESSION OF ANGER
SOMETIMES BE NECESSARY?

ANGER
MISUNDERSTOOD

I witnessed an interesting intervention at a roundtable discussion on race relations in South Africa in Johannesburg in early 2015. The participants agreed that the record of discussion would not identify who had made which comment so as to create a space that was as conducive to honesty as was possible among relative strangers. And that worked. But one moment during the discussion has stuck with me.

The moderator for the discussions was, in one sense, a perfect choice. She had an excellent tone and a sense of calm that immediately made the space comfortable, inclusive and inviting. She has what one might lazily call 'a soft touch' but she is not soft on the issues. She cares deeply for social justice, and the enduring evidence of racism bothers her intensely, as it does many of us. I liked her as the moderator, knowing secretly we have enormous overlapping consensus in our world views, but appreciating her capacity to make even racist Afrikaners feel they can safely express their views in the space provided.

But I deliberately described these qualities as perfect 'in one sense'. I had never thought critically about ground rules for a discussion until something happened in that room. Everyone had been polite, waiting their turn, not interrupting each other, listening actively or pretending to do so, but for the occasional hint of disagreeing body language here and there. A burly Afrikaans man – call him Fanie – then spoke for the first time. He can't be criticised for being burly. Or having a booming voice. But the impact of his physicality was jarring, I have to confess, because it felt like whiteness announcing itself through a loudhailer, not helped by the content of what he had to say, which was essentially that we were all colour-blind and see inner beauty and the real and only culprit interrupting our march towards Non-Racial Nirvana was – of course – the black-led ANC government.

And then he stopped, looking pleased to have announced what he probably regarded as an incontestable truism. No doubt it must be shocking when people challenge what you regard as truth, especially if you are not used to honest interaction with people of very different linguistic, racial, class, geographic and other social markers to the ones criss-crossing your body. That is precisely what he got: disagreement – politely and carefully articulated – from a black woman (call her Nomsa) of gentle stature at the other side of the room. Her intervention upset him instantly. Just like that, he started barking at her while she was still speaking! The room was in shock. It was the first outburst, the first interruption since the rules of engagement had been carefully laid out and role-modelled by the moderator. Fanie incurred everyone's wrath, and a number of us muttered that he ought to, as political comrades might say to each other, arrest himself. He did briefly, and then like an automaton, just snapped again. The chair had to pull him back and remind everyone of the agreed ground rules that were a necessary condition for us to be able to make headway in the search for answers to questions in which we had a mutual interest in pursuing, carefully and thoughtfully. He managed to calm down a little bit and the roundtable discussion continued, and not all was lost.

I hasten to add, of course, that I do not believe that the outburst was innocent or the social equivalent of temporary insanity. Nor is he a machine that malfunctioned. That kind of description would be disingenuous and would let him off the hook too quickly. For one thing, he is a confident, healthy, grown ass man who has a lot of agency that he exercises as he chooses to; for another, this was the familiar behaviour of someone unconscious of their internalised sense of entitlement. Fanie felt a sense of entitlement to speak, entitlement to have the last word, entitlement not to be shown up or doubted. It was deliberate behaviour powered by the unreflective privilege of white male dominance.

Fanie wasn't malfunctioning. He was performing a habit, that of travelling through this world of ours assuming that his world view is objective reality. Until a confident black woman, Nomsa, deflated his false belief. It was a privilege to witness such a timely rupture of culpably unconscious bad behaviour.

But if you think that is the highlight of the story, I have more in store. Just when I thought order had been restored, nicely and rightly so, another black woman – a brilliant, young academic and activist talent – put up her hand to take us back to the incident that had played out earlier. Let's call her Joyce.

Joyce said – with ironic but tactful calm, given what she was in fact about to say – that she had a problem with the ground rules that had been established. She said that it appeared as if the ground rules were neutral in the sense of helping everyone feel welcome, and so enabled everyone to participate freely and with dignity, but in fact things were not that simple. Ground rules were not neutral devices designed to get dialogue flowing. She didn't want to be calm about racism and colonialism and its modern-day manifestations like pervasive white privilege, as performed by Fanie earlier. Joyce wanted to be angry, and to come into this roundtable space angry, because the nature and effects of colonialism and related modern evils like apartheid required not just a calm response, but also an expression of anger.

I am somewhat embellishing the word choices here, but that is the core sentiment she expressed, and it hit me like a ton of bricks. I saw the very idea of uncontested, polite rules of engagement in a new light.

Joyce concluded by saying that the ground rules favoured the *beneficiary* of racism and colonialism, and privileged their desire not to be pelted by emotional bombs. These ground rules were, for that reason, also a form of policing the emotions of racism's victims. So while the logic of ground rules, if you do not reflect on their impact carefully, makes sense intuitively – they are necessary to make progress in dialogue – the truth is that, regardless of this praiseworthy intention, it is the bully or perpetrator who benefits more from a space in which the victim is told to mind their anger, their tears, or any other affective state.

I think this critique of the ground rules by Joyce is compelling. It focuses our attention on the unintended consequence of setting up 'safe spaces' for disagreeing people to meet and talk.

And that is what I meant by the moderator being perfect 'in one sense'. There is another sense, given what Joyce has argued, in which the moderator was not perfect. Like all of us who moderate these kinds of events, we hardly ever reflect on the effect of the rules of engagement we lay out at the beginning of such a session. And, sure, if you are facilitating a strategy session for a company, these kinds of rules are fine, or at a conference for an industry body, perhaps. But here, in a forum for social dialogue, the very processes that you put in place can reproduce the kinds of hegemony that you are trying to get participants to discuss. I am grateful to Joyce for these insights.

Unfortunately, the moderator didn't know what to do with Joyce's intervention, and continued facilitating a discussion on the substantive issues that had emerged. As I chewed on Joyce's remarks in the days after that roundtable, it all reminded me of what I have been wanting to articulate about anger more generally. Her critique of rules of engagement that favour the bully dovetails with a public defence of anger that is overdue.

Joyce wasn't, of course, only talking about how best to run a roundtable that has people in one space who disagree deeply about many things. I think the real conversation that was supposed to be opened up, but which wasn't central to the aim of that gathering, is the place of emotion in dialogue. There is a gross tendency, in my view, to regard the expression of strong emotion, especially anger, as a sign of someone losing control or reducing the prospects of mutual respect and the prospects of disagreeing individuals finding each other.

This view is as unconvincing as it is popular. In the rest of this essay I want to offer a calm defence of anger. Anger has, for too long now, been needlessly misunderstood, as if he who is the calmest is necessarily the most rational or necessarily the most self-reflective or necessarily the most pragmatic. These are myths that need shattering. Anger is not only sometimes allowed; I think, in some contexts, the expression of anger might even be necessary, and praiseworthy.

I CAN EMOTE IF I WANT TO

If you have been extensively bullied by someone – think of social media trolling, physical bullying in the playground, sex pests in the office, etc. – it would be hugely draining, emotionally, for someone to ask you to meet the troll, the schoolboy bully, the sex pest, in order to 'talk things through' and to do so politely so that everyone 'can be heard'. This request for you to please remain calm assumes, in effect, that there is an equal entitlement to respect between you and the perpetrator.

But this surely, despite being well meaning and perhaps driven from restorative-justice principles, has got to be warped. The bully, the troll or the sex pest cannot be entitled to a comfortable space. If the bully's victim or survivor wants to afford them an undeserved opportunity to be heard calmly, fully, actively, then fine. But to demand of a victim that they agree to such ground rules is to compound the suffering they have already experienced at the hands of the perpetrator. No rape victim should have the burden of having to be friendly to her rapist. That makes no moral sense.

For Joyce, what was at stake at that roundtable discussion in Johannesburg was her entitlement to choose how she wants to express her experience of racism. Her emotion should not be policed. Neither by black people who do not care to get angry or regard it as useless to do so, or by white people who think that it is an unhelpful move to be angry when a racist reaches out to you at last. Magnanimity isn't compulsory. It is solely up to Joyce to decide how she responds in that context.

TWO PURPOSES OF ANGER

Expressing anger can be an appropriate exhibition of moral outrage at that which is broken in society. I observed a drunk male student at a pub in Grahamstown disgustingly trying to touch random female students inappropriately as they walked up to the bar. He clearly did not know them. They were objects of his sexual lust and, with drunken slurs, he taunted them and made them very uncomfortable until, mercifully, a friend of his intervened.

I felt myself getting angry and, thinking of what to say, I got ready to intervene. The anger I felt manifested in my entire body, which got rather tense, and my mind focused on him. My heart was racing. It was not, as anger is often deliberately mischaracterised by those scared of its place in social and political life, rampant anger that was about to lead to a fight and me being on the front page of the *Grocott's Mail*. It was controlled anger, and in fact while *feeling* this anger filling my body, I was still able to think clearly, judging him … all the while watching this misogyny play out, and reasoning morally about how I should respond.

My anger served at least two purposes, I would argue: it was evidence of a moral conscience being activated (I hope); and, secondly, it propelled me to potentially act, and so it had a motivating effect on me to try to amend what was socially broken in front of my eyes. And I think each of these elements of anger, on their own, justify anger.

Anger as an expression of moral disapproval is important in our social lives. It's a bit like a pain receptor. If you are unable to feel pain, you will not know when your body is broken, and needs to be mended. You might simply one day collapse, and it could then be too late to revive you, because you never attended to what was initially a small problem. Being able to feel physical pain is an important part of surviving and an important part of living well. The body needs some way of knowing when all is not okay with it.

Our moral well-being is the same. If there were moral sins in our society being committed, but no one ever felt certain moral emotions, then we would be in danger of not always noticing when a situation is morally broken. We are not robots or wholly intellectual creatures. We also use instinct, which is why

156

a feeling of physical pain is useful to us, because it instinctively gets us to take action.

With morality, it is just as useful that we feel certain moral emotions, and that these signal to us that all is not morally well. One difference with physical pain is that a moral emotion isn't just a trigger to motivate us to act. Once we feel the emotion, like anger, we can also express that anger, and the mere expression of anger has moral value, regardless of what might happen thereafter. This is because the expression of anger conveys the message that someone messed up, morally. It is an indictment of their behaviour.

And so if Joyce wants not only to feel anger but also to express it when she encounters a racist, the moral value of showing your anger is a form of calling them out, morally. Sure, there are no guarantees the bigot will give a damn, reflect on your anger, or even come to accept they did wrong, let alone change their behaviour, but our moral lives do not just consist of actions that can bring about guaranteed change. Part of what it means to be the kind of social creatures with emotional and moral qualities that we are, is that we also care for expressions of how we feel.

It's important for a moral community to express disapproval even if someone doesn't change their ways. Imagine, for example, we only enforced legal rules if there were guarantees that someone would change their ways? We'd hardly ever lock someone up or fine them. But of course one of the functions of the law is that it allows society to express disapproval of wrongdoing before we even ask questions about whether the expression of disapproval would make the world a safer place. Similarly, moral disapproval of racism, in the form of an expression of anger, is an important social signal that wrongdoing isn't acceptable.

That said, there is a practical benefit to getting angry, and even showing it. Anger can sometimes propel us to act so that we correct that which is socially broken. I think it is far less likely that I would step in and rebuke a sexist pig at the bar as a bystander if I had no affective component to my response to the situation I was witnessing. But when your blood is boiling, as the saying usefully goes, you ready yourself to act, and that isn't a bad thing. If you were emotionally inert, you'd probably only ever be a bystander to all sorts of injustices around you. The functional value of anger shouldn't be underestimated.

This is why I think, in some cases, it might even be necessary, if not compulsory, to get angry. If someone was grossly violated, like having been assaulted, and he wasn't angry at the perpetrator, we would find that odd. Of course, the person may draw on deep personal, religious or some other inner resources at his disposal to deal with his experiences. We don't cope in the same way when we are violated, and we don't have the same view about these kinds of experiences; even our moral attitudes to assault may differ. So one must make allowance for this.

But barring the most exceptional kind of forgiveness-centred approach to life, if someone never ever got angry when they were wronged, we would be right to suspect that there was something amiss in their moral life, or at least that their unusual response to personal injury required explaining. If rights that you are entitled to by virtue of being a human being are trampled on, you ought to get angry, at least sometimes.

I am not for a moment trying to imply that one cannot do important work in fighting racism unless you get angry. Calm conversation and spaces equally friendly to all interlocutors can help people to see the world differently and facilitate effective collaboration between perpetrators and victims. I accept that. What I do not accept is that the expression of anger should be parodied, thought of as embarrassing, and regarded as never, ever useful or appropriate. I do fear, however, that while many people would agree that we can dismantle aspects of the architecture of racism calmly, fewer people regard an expression of strong emotion like anger as *obviously* defensible, let alone sometimes obligatory as the only way to demonstrate your refusal to be disrespected.

This happened to journalist and writer Rebecca Davis, and other women, on Twitter, several times. After lengthy attempts to engage sexist pigs calmly, logically and in an evidence-sensitive manner, on such emotionally fraught debates as whether or not some women falsely accuse men of rape, or whether women should 'take care' of how they dress and where they hang out to 'avoid' being raped, Rebecca understandably grew impatient with the barracking and trolling. Eventually she simply told one of these scumbag to fuck off.

My goodness, the backlash was insane, but instructive. Essentially she was portrayed as an irrational chick who could not control her emotions because, *ag-ja*-well, we all know how *mos* emotional chicks can get, especially these angry lesbian feminist Nazi types like Rebecca. That was the message and abuse expressed with openness in full view of the world. It takes a special amount of arrogance to have no shame about publicly flaunting this misogyny. Normal, flawed human beings at least fear the possibility of reputational damage, but not these sexist trolls. They are used to having their world view affirmed everywhere they traverse.

The question is whether Rebecca lost her cool when she told them to fuck off. I don't think so. And not only, by the way, because she had already exhausted polite conversation. She didn't need to do that first before being allowed to get angry and to express that anger. Unless you are engaging someone like a child, a mentally ill patient or someone who is intellectually and morally underdeveloped, you are not obliged to take extra care to make them see the warped nature of the misogynistic views they express or attitudes they display. The expression of the anger is adequately justified by the mere fact that misogyny triggered it. And the anger so expressed is an indication of moral outrage that you feel, an example of a conscience that is active.

Besides, I have yet to meet more than a negligibly tiny number of bigots – of any variety – who are serious about self-examination. They do not care about truth. Truth is not a value that is central to their reasoning habits, let alone their moral life. They just want to hate. And they want to preserve their power in a society where the distribution of power is invariably skewed in their favour. If that is what you are up against, revising your lessons from first-year formal logic tutorials is an intellectually cute but politically impotent way to proceed. Because they do not share your commitment to eliminating false or odious beliefs from their belief system. So why waste energy when you can simply walk away, or say, 'FUCK OFF!' Try it. (Right now. Have a practice run before someone walks in on you. It is really liberating … isn't it?)

TWO FINAL THOUGHTS

I suspect some people might accept that anger can have moral and practical value *sometimes*, but would want to guard against a wholesale promotion of anger being expressed left, right and centre, fearing that it could actually, more often than not, undermine the possibility of people finding each other in dialogue.

So if we go back to Joyce's critique of so-called safe spaces, the fear would be that, while nothing that Joyce said is particularly unconvincing, it would be better to be calm and polite if that means a chance of the burly white Afrikaans guy seeing the world differently, perhaps, after the roundtable. Isn't the aim, after all, to bring about change in interpersonal relations, and institutional reform? If it means anger playing second fiddle to enabling real change, then it is just prudent not to encourage anger, and maybe even to discourage it.

Or we could frame this advice as a challenge: if Joyce exercised her entitlement to be pissed, and to express being pissed off, then what?

I am slightly conflicted about this. It seems like a usefully pragmatic view to take. The offer of possible material, maybe even structural, change is a juicy incentive to ask me to check my emotions. I guess it is a bit like, in political terms, asking black negotiators at the Convention for a Democratic South Africa to keep calm rather than getting angry because that would more likely lead to an outcome in which the humanity of all people is affirmed, and entrenched in a new constitutional dispensation.

But the problem here is that this crude pragmatism really doesn't take seriously what the expression of anger, as I have explained it, is about, morally *and practically*. If you get that anger is a legitimate move in dialogue, then it must not be eliminated by other ways of bringing about systemic change. We should rather see all of these tools as different and complementary implements in a box from which you can choose depending on the situational requirements and the judgement call being made by the victims of racism. The victims alone must own the method of dealing with racism's legacy. If, say, Joyce chooses to be angry and the Afrikaans *boytjie* storms out of the room, that is fine! That is still Joyce's choice.

Because what is gained here, in that scenario, is respect for her autonomy for the first time, wholeheartedly, in the history of racism. You can't trample on someone's dignity, and then think you can make up for it by paternalistically telling him or her how to behave in the world now that you are done trampling on them. If the process of reducing the effects of racism is clumsy, not linear, a case of two steps forward and one back,

162

that is not the end of the world. It is critical for the restoration of the victim's dignity that they alone choose that path. And the beneficiaries of privilege must show some humility here, as philosopher Samantha Vice has argued. (I think I hastily rebutted this idea as unfair on white people in a previous engagement with her. I finally get, I think, what she meant.)

As I argued in an earlier essay, I am not grateful that you want to work on your bigotry. You are not doing me a favour. You are simply doing what is morally *decent*. And if you do it with that motive, then you ought to know that seeing your bigotry or privilege for what it is for the first time in your life does not mean you must now be rewarded for not being Steve Hofmeyr. You should still be humble, and not instruct black activists and black people more generally to be careful of alienating whites who could help them chip away at institutional and structural racism faster than if we work apart.

In other words, that abrasive Afrikaans *oke* who was on the brink of working on his privilege until Joyce shouted at him, is not let off the hook if he runs away during the break and his personal work stops, and he is back in the racism closet. Joyce's anger is permitted. And he simply failed, morally. If he wants to be rewarded for trying but not staying the course when Joyce gets angry in the context of the huge ongoing effects racism has on Joyce, then I say to that *oke*, 'Fuck off!'

ARE COLOURED PEOPLE BLACK?

WHY ARE SOME OF US ASHAMED
OF BEING COLOURED?

WHAT ARE THE DIFFERENCES BETWEEN
'COLOURED PEOPLE'?

FOR COLOURED
PEOPLE ONLY

I do not find coloured people interesting. I do not know how to write about coloured people. I do not know what to say about coloured people. And I feel bad about feeling this way. Because I feel compelled to be able to write about coloured people, to have strong feelings about coloured identity, and have something to offer, in my writing and other work, to coloured readers, radio listeners or television viewers.

I feel compelled to write about coloured people because I have coloured identity thrust upon me. It is interesting that, despite the weak biological basis for race categories, there are invented identities one cannot, it would seem, choose or reject. There may be many labels hurled my way – coloured, mixed race, so-called coloured, brown – but South Africans fluent in the racist classification system perfected by the apartheid state *know* I am coloured. *I* know I am coloured.

And yet, at the same time, many of us want to reject the idea that race is an essential trait, a biological truth. How do we square the fact that race is biological nonsense with the reality that we do, however, have racialised lived identities? And where do coloured people fit into this awkward racial topography? First, it is important to get to the bottom of my own deep discomfort with this entire 'coloured debate'.

COLOURED IDENTITY AND SHAME

I am black. I self-identify politically as black. I am also coloured. Yes, it is confusing. I reconcile, for myself, these statements as consistent with each other by thinking of myself as 'culturally coloured but politically black'. That description seems to best fit my lived experiences while respecting my agency to be immersed in the politics of identity and race as I choose to do.

When I say I am 'culturally coloured', I acknowledge descriptive truths about the coloured community; that, for better or worse, through apartheid policies rooted in colonial heritage, coloured people, as an imagined people, came into social and political existence. It was messy, it was violent, and it was often irrational and inconsistent stuff on the part of the apartheid state. And it was always immoral, and in service of a racist project: that of preserving and furthering white supremacist attitudes and artefacts.

The irrationality of this constructed coloured community played out even in my family. My paternal grandfather had a brother who cut ties with the family by successfully getting himself reclassified as white by the apartheid state. On my maternal side, the family was moved from our house in a part of Grahamstown that was suddenly designated for 'black Africans' only. Hundreds of towns and cities have their own District Six forced-removal stories and histories. All of this violence found expression and fake legitimacy in apartheid laws such as the Population Registration Act – which my great uncle relied on to be reclassified as white – and the Group Areas Act, which rendered lawful the violent forced removals.

Out of immoral and violent apartheid policies, however, an imagined community became an actual community. We speak Afrikaans. We lived in, and mostly still live in, communities that are almost exclusively Afrikaans, and mostly with coloured people or people of mixed heritage or whatever terminology you are most comfortable with if you are a member of this imagined community that became an actual community.

Coloured people share a common history rooted in this evil anti-black racism project of dividing black people by creating a 'non-white' hierarchy of races, and even compelling them to live apart. So our community origins are painful. But the conundrum is that we now have a history and shared memory, horrid memories and cultural tropes you would normally find in communities that did not come about through such forced political projects as the apartheid government.

I cannot possibly imagine what it must be like to find out, as an adult, that a hospital had made a mistake and gave your parents the wrong baby to take home. In the meantime, you have developed familial bonds with your siblings and parents and they with you. You *are* a family. You have a shared history, including the newly discovered historic fact that you do not share genetic material, and you have shared memories, joyous ones and the pains of growing up that everyone goes through. What do you do? Deny these bonds because an original historic fact about how it all started is an injustice?

The origins of the coloured community, for me, share aspects of this analogy. There are two differences of course: an innocent hospital swop is regrettable but not the worst moral sin if the error was a rare and unintended one, whereas the apartheid project was inherently immoral and inherently violent; the second difference is that racial identities are weird, biologically – because, on the one hand, although races do not exist in biology, racial traits are biological traits. After all, my skin colour and my hair texture are biological facts. When we look into the lineage of coloured people, not every coloured person or every coloured community is the result of miscegenation. So coloured identity is a mix of social and political imagination, but a construction that piggybacks on bits of biology and shared, even if varying, genealogies, depending on your family tree.

What is undeniable, however, is that many of us who are coloured are profoundly self-conscious of the painful historic basis upon which we came about as a group. Which brings me to my own shame.

An older cousin of mine encouraged me to think about what it is that is lurking below my declared reluctance to give coloured people, and coloured identity, greater prominence in my writing, and my general reluctance to think about my own heritage. I can't even tell you much about the history of my own family.

I'm tempted to think, as I did in conversation with my cousin, that maybe it is shame that drives my discomfort. I suspect that's probably right, but I am honestly not sure. It can also be rather easy, and melodramatic, to boldly declare that one feels shame or that one is ashamed of who one is, or where one comes from. Shame isn't easy to get a grip on. So I neither want to run away from my own shame, nor do I want to induce false tears in myself or you by self-diagnosing this stuff as *shame*. There are no easy answers here, and lots of complexity to live with, and constantly explore, and sometimes ignore so that life can continue.

Isn't shame an emotion I would feel if I were not just embarrassed about a state of affairs, but also, in addition, if I felt that I did not meet my own or society's standards? Similarly, when I feel ashamed of someone or something – maybe feeling ashamed of my friend or of my government – the very meaning of the shame felt in that context is a kind of self-flagellation that says, 'My friend fell short of acceptable social norms/My state fell short of what was reasonably expected of it'. Shame is very powerful. One can be embarrassed – like when you accidently fart in company – without feeling ashamed. Shame is a powerful and important moral emotion. It can help you check your own behaviour. And to become a better person if you falter. The inability to feel shame, or to ever be ashamed, would be a moral failure.

But here's the thing. It is also possible, of course, to be ashamed of yourself or someone else or a state of affairs when you should not be ashamed. We are not always accurate in our assessment of whether or not we have fallen short of social standards. Sometimes the standards we imagine are ridiculous and should be rejected. If a woman gets abused by her partner and eventually digs deep enough to leave him, she might feel ashamed of having been abused or being a divorced woman, say. In this kind of context the source of shame is a set of social norms that are simply outdated but tragically can still mess up our psychological well-being if we are not able to resist the influence of bad social standards.

My grandfather attempted to make my mom feel shame for thinking of getting a divorce from my dad. A huge cause of delay in getting on with leaving her violent marriage was the very real shame she felt, as a good Catholic, for thinking of exiting her marriage. My mom's shame was misplaced. And the misogyny of the church, and my grandfather's preoccupation both with Catholicism's maxims, and the family reputation in the community, were ridiculous constraints on my mother's agency. Fortunately, being the fantastically hard-headed woman that she was, she took her own decision and got divorced anyway. But these kinds of cases often demonstrate misplaced shame.

I think there is a sense in which I feel misplaced shame about the coloured community. The coloured community has not fallen short of social standards. Seemingly shameful facts about the coloured community are simply a reflection of the shameful legacy of colonialism and apartheid. So my cousin is, I suspect, right. I do feel ashamed of being coloured. But my feelings are completely misplaced, and I need to find ways of slowly eliminating this internalised oppression. It has too many odious consequences. Because in discussing these consequences in the context of South African racism, it's important, while the confession continues, to be clear about how the shame in me operates, and manifests itself, before arresting the logic of misplaced self-shame.

The most familiar experience is hiding your roots. Sometimes this is literally so, in the case of your hair! I am, in my case, referring to where you live. There is a lot of alcoholism in my community and general poverty. Fighting between people, in our families or neighbours' yards, can happen at any time. There is a lot I love about my community – the bits I refer to as 'cultural identity' which I explore shortly – but a trip through the geography of my childhood isn't a happy one. The thought of bussing my friends off to where I grew up is hard. This, of course, is not unique to the coloured community in one sense. Undignified poverty is a fact of most black South African life.

But I could never shake off the feeling that we coloured people are far more class homogenous than other racial groups. We are, with only slight exaggeration, *essentially* a downtrodden lot. That's not a moral claim or diss. I mean that to be a description of the socio-economic horrors in our communities that allow for little diversity. Sure, some coloured people end up being poets or authors or top-ranking businesspeople or politicians or civil servants.

I am most certainly not making the absurd and self-evidently false claim that being coloured guarantees a life of misery. But our relationships with our communities do not neatly track comprehensive facts. That's not how lived reality works. Whether grounded in falsehood or not, in my head, and heart, as Eusebius McKaiser, I have always thought of the coloured community in very melancholic terms. And it stems from an association of 'coloured' with 'downtrodden'. It doesn't help, of course, that in places like the Western Cape and the Northern Cape, you find some of the world's highest levels of foetal alcohol syndrome, and disastrously endemic drug addiction and rife gangsterism on the Cape Flats. These are the images and words that I associate with my coloured identity. It is these things that fuel my shame about my people.

Yet, of course, these feelings are completely ridiculous. But knowing something intellectually doesn't instantly change how you feel. It takes time. It takes practice. It takes deliberate effort to forge a new relationship with your own self, and your community. That is work I have not done, and frankly work I have avoided doing. Because self-shame is that debilitating. It is self-shame that makes many AIDS patients die unnecessary deaths. It is self-shame that stops us, that stops me, from forging and enjoying stunning, new, renewed relationships with my family, community, and *myself*.

The reason, by the way, that my shame is ridiculous is that I have not violated social norms by being coloured. Nor has the coloured community fallen short of acceptable social norms. So there is no healthy shame to be felt about being coloured. There is only unhealthy self-shame. And the power and hold that unhealthy self-shame can have over any of us isn't easily dealt with. But staring it in the face and calling it out for what it is, is a good start.

Objectively speaking, the social ills that are prevalent in coloured communities across the country were not chosen by us. The structure of poverty has a history that predates any coloured person alive today. We were the bastard children of colonial wars and violence that continued under apartheid. The state underinvested in our communities, as it did in black African communities, and so opportunities for flourishing were rare. In that kind of environment, failure and depression have a better chance of thriving than a Trevor Manuel or a Zoë Wicomb emerging. That doesn't mean coloured people do not have agency. If anything, we often do not take seriously enough the agency we have by virtue of being human.

But only an ahistorical fool would deny the material impact that structural injustices have on the lives of individuals. No one's 'agency' can magically change social facts like apartheid laws that reserve jobs for some and not for others. The violence, drug addiction, unhealthy masculinities, high unemployment rates and other facts about coloured communities are not reasons to feel shame or be ashamed of being coloured. They are simply a small number of facts in a country's larger history of anti-black racism. And that is why my lifelong feelings of shame about these community truths are misplaced. They have no rational basis, upon reflection.

THE HARM OF PARTIAL TRUTHS

Another cousin of mine challenged my internalised belief that very few coloured people excel, and that the dominant narrative of a typical coloured life is one of unfulfilled potential. She suggested that maybe I had always been lazy about learning about brilliant coloured people who have contributed to our society in many areas of life from the arts to politics, education, business and more.

I think she probably has a point. I struggle to rattle off a list of names that could make for a whole 13-part series on television about the incredible, positive contribution that coloured people have made to this country. That is my own ignorance. And that is one of the consequences of self-shame. It leads to a refusal to see, to explore and to find out more about yourself and your community. You simply refuse to go there, in more ways than one. And that impoverishes your own self, and your community, especially when you occupy a position of influence as a writer and broadcaster. This new awareness means nothing unless future output from these fingers of mine demonstrates that I took seriously the harm of partial truths about coloured people that I accept I have been a purveyor of.

I still think of myself as 'culturally coloured' and have no shame attached to that self-identity. Yet, here too I have knowledge gaps that beg to be filled. There's a rich history of cuisine, for example, that coloured communities have, which in part reflects the different histories of different families and communities all loosely grouped together under the ultimately vague label of 'coloured people'. But it is food, drinks, in-jokes, growing up together and other banal daily lived realities that give me my own sense of 'cultural identity'. As much as my now English middle-class life separates me from my working-class Afrikaans relatives and early childhood friends, in profound ways, at the same time the mere sight of an old friend, when I am back in Grahamstown, can result in cultural recognition, instant familiarity and shared memory: the glue that binds us as a coloured community even as we grapple with our place under the South African sky.

There are some conversations I cannot have with my family because my life took a different turn from theirs. My coconut, privileged self knows many parts of South Africa and the world that they do not. My sisters, for example, do not have white or black African friends. That is true of most of my family. I do. That alone differentiates us politically. I adopt a black political identity and posture born out of, in part, cross-racial solidarity with other black people who have been victims of anti-black racism. My sisters self-identify as coloured, both culturally and politically.

But despite our different politics, we share the cultural

connections, even as I still have work to do to understand the details of cultural heritage. But, what's clear though, is that just as there are conversations, politically, I cannot have with my relatives, there are also ways of being coloured that my white and black African friends would not get. A lot of my laughter with my dad, for example, cannot be explained to white folks or black Africans without some translation. Coloured people would get us instantly. Just as there is a grammar of whiteness, so too is there a coloured cultural grammar. And much work needs to be done to archive, explore, debate, and narrate these contested ways of being coloured.

AREN'T WE ALL JUST BLACK?

There is one debate about coloured identity that I do have a strong view on. It is the arrogance with which other people want to impose on coloured people what they should think of themselves. The latest person to do so is the African National Congress's Gwede Mantashe who has said that coloured people must accept that they are also black. This infuriates me.

It is not the place of Mantashe, or any person who is black African, to prescribe to coloured communities how they should self-identify. It is a debate that must take place among coloured people because identity runs deep, and it is the shared experiences and histories of coloured people that must inform how they – how we – want to self-identify. To impose political identities on coloured people from outside the community is to rob us of our agency to think through these complex moral and political issues that are implicated in the history of coloured people.

I have experienced this arrogance several times. Try host a radio debate, for example, about coloured people and within seconds you will have some black African listeners call in and say, with utter confidence like someone thinking they are expressing a blatantly obvious truism, 'We are all black! Coloured people are black! Why are we even discussing this topic?!' That kind of remark rolls off people's tongues like white listeners who respond to radio debates about racism by shouting their own presumed truisms, 'We are all human! Races do not exist! Why are we even discussing this topic?'

Hold on, South Africans. We need to, as writer Sisonke Msimang put so well, learn to 'live in complexity'. Of course races are not biologically stable concepts. But that does not change the history of racism, nor the fact that we have racialised identities as a result of the history of colonialism and apartheid. We cannot wish these lived experiences away. It is possible for race to be a social construction and still be a concept that operates on the world in the most powerful ways possible. Indeed, that is exactly the history of this country.

So, firstly, we need to disabuse ourselves of the fantasy that races do not exist and we should not talk about race. Races exist as social realities, and that is why racism was possible at all. To eliminate racism totally, we need to accept that racial identities continue. And that these identities remain a defining fault line in post-apartheid South Africa.

Secondly, black African and coloured people have, in general, very dodgy attitudes to one another. Many coloured people I know have racist attitudes to black Africans. Many black Africans I know have racist attitudes to coloured people. And many have an incredible number of false, and harmful, stereotypes they associate with one another. That is the legacy of racism. Apartheid was so powerful before we dismantled it politically, that it succeeded in driving a wedge between us as blacks and coloureds. We have work to do to defeat the social consequences of apartheid.

That, in part, is why I hate it when a black African caller wants to shut down a conversation about coloured identity by saying that we are all black. Because it is insincere! Mantashe, too, is insincere! If the ANC took seriously the fact that we are all black, then Trevor Manuel would likely have been president by now. There is a glass ceiling on your career inside the ANC if you're not black African. That is not anything the ANC should be ashamed of just yet. It is a reflection of what apartheid did to us: it divided us. And we have not yet closed those divisions. It is also the reason why coloured voters in the Western Cape do not have a natural home in either the ANC or the DA. Because apartheid left us feeling like we're essentially not black, and not white, and we associate those parties with racial essences.

My grandfather swore, in his old age, and voting for the first time in 1994, that he would not vote for the ANC because he doesn't trust blacks. 'Look what they did to Rhodesia!' he told my 15-year-old self. This stuff has not vanished. And I bet you many black Africans who say that coloureds must accept that they are black themselves display odious attitudes to coloured people. There is a necessary, difficult and overdue conversation that coloured and black African people must have about how anti-black racism resulted in us 'othering' one another. That discussion cannot be silenced by Mantashe imposing black identity on coloured people who do not want it, or do not feel that they have yet been heard on the issue of their own alienation from the new South Africa. Sadly, Mantashe's view underscores why coloured voters are floating voters. We are not at home anywhere politically.

FINAL THOUGHTS

The way forward is to accept that there are no truisms. There are no easy victories to be had. Only long, hard and difficult conversations to initiate. I have, for example, referred to myself as 'culturally coloured'. Many coloured people hate the word 'coloured'. Some prefer 'so-called coloured' or 'brown' or 'person of mixed descent' or … other possibilities. What's in a name? A lot. And that debate alone merits a self-standing dialogue within the coloured community.

A second discussion is about whether or not it is tactically and politically sensible to simply subsume our lived experiences under the term 'black'. Should we take up Mantashe's advice and self-identify, simply, as black? Isn't that the ultimate middle finger to show the ghost of Hendrik Verwoerd? I do not know. I cop out of a definitive view by thinking of myself as politically black and culturally coloured, of course. But what does it mean to be 'politically black'? That, too, requires a self-standing dialogue.

A third discussion must explore the impact that shame has on us as individuals and as a community. It chokes us. It stops us from doing work we need to do. That, too, requires a self-standing dialogue.

Finally, it is overdue that we archive and publicly celebrate and know the men and women who are loosely referred to as 'coloured'. Our history needs to be known popularly, our similarities understood and differences across the country cherished. And my nephews and nieces need to be able to know the contribution of coloured people to this country in a way in which I, shamefully, do not.

CAN DIFFERENT RACES HAVE UNIQUE
RELATIONSHIPS WITH THE SAME FOOD AND MUSIC?

DO WE FEAR GROUP DIFFERENCES?

IS A SEARCH FOR COMMONALITY AMONG
RACE GROUPS FUTILE?

AT LEAST ALLOW US BEETROOT SALAD, JUDY BOUCHER AND BLACK TAX, PLEASE?

BEETROOT FOR MY DEARLY DEPARTED

Nothing says 'Welcome home!' quite as deliciously as a plate of Sunday lunch with seven colours. It might be pumpkin, roast chicken, rice, gravy, spinach, potatoes, cauliflower with white sauce, lamb stew and, ah, the most homely of them all – beetroot salad, or, as some simply say, beet salad or beet. My mom called it 'beetroot salad' and any other description is just plain weird to me. Because Mom is always right. Or … most of the time. She certainly wasn't right when she *bliksem*-ed me with a hairbrush for messing up her pot plant. She didn't even bother to first take out my sisters' hair still stuck in that green hairbrush. When it comes to cooking, though, Mom is always right – from how and what to cook, to how to name each item on your plate of Sunday lunch.

When your food swims in beetroot salad, red juices infusing everything else on the plate, then you know you're truly home, far away from the suburbs of Joburg where you might eat Woolies' packaged meals, even on Good Friday. I am not sure what the origins of the 'seven colours' description is, to be honest. I have on several occasions tried to count the colours on my plate, and I do not once recall the number to be exactly seven. But, who am I to be cheeky and behave like a clever black when I can simply get on with the business of eating palm-licking home-cooked food (after praying with the family, of course, despite my flight from religion)?

The other occasions I associate with beetroot salad are funerals. I think black people would have a massive bun fight if you made us choose which occasion beetroot salad *most* reminds us of – Sunday lunch or funerals? A funeral is not a funeral if beetroot salad does not make an appearance. Mrs Ball's doesn't have to come to a black funeral. But, without beetroot salad, your dearly beloved could not possibly have departed dearly. Beetroot at a funeral is necessary for closure.

I secretly hated the taste of beetroot! I still do. I'm just glad Mom isn't around to read this confession. I find it bland, and though some aunties' beetroot salad clearly wasn't as edible as my mom's, I have always compared beetroot salads by degrees of inedibility, rather than by degrees of mouthgasmic-ness. If there is too much vinegar in it, it is particularly bad. If there is just the right amount of vinegar in it, you can get on with eating it. My mom's *obviously* had just the right amount of vinegar in it, yet even then I had a tactic for how to eat it: I always made sure my spoon contained about one-third beetroot salad and two-thirds of some warm, yummy food. Not only did that make sure I didn't only taste beetroot, but it also had the advantage of ensuring the beetroot taste could be dominated by rich-flavoured lasagne, for example. If the food was hot, the gastronomic juxtaposition of hot lasagne and cold beetroot salad was sheer genius on my part.

Beetroot is an unavoidable family nuisance like your drunk uncle at the wedding. (Mind you, some of us have drunk aunts at a funeral, but now *ja*.) Nonetheless, I enjoyed watching Mom make the beetroot salad. She would cut off the long stems of the beetroot, boil a pot of water, and put in the uhm … I guess you'd call them beetroot heads? I don't know, but you put them in the hot water to cook for a long while. Eventually, when they were cooked, she'd wait for the water to cool before taking them out. I think, and hope my sisters won't pierce a wobbly memory here, she would peel them – or not – but what she most definitely did thereafter I have never forgotten. She grated the cold beetroot heads into a glass bowl; grated them like you would carrots, into little flat, finger-length strips. And then – her other secret – she would add just enough sugar so it wasn't obviously sweet, but so that the sugar could wrestle nicely with the inherent blandness of the root, and then she would add vinegar, before popping it into the fridge to chillax before we went to church.

Because Mom grated the beetroot, as an adult I find it near impossible to eat beetroot salad if the beetroot pieces are chunks. Because my mom's way of making it is surely the only way that beetroot salad can be made, no? I still frown and shake my head in shops when I see something even weirder than large chunks of home-made beetroot: some shops sell bottles of beetroot salad containing neatly, evenly sliced, disc-shaped pieces of beetroot salad *in a glass bottle*. WTF? Just as weird as Woolies now selling samp and beans in a tin. *Umngqush*! That's just not right. You don't buy or sell beetroot salad. Ever. Not if you're a respectable black family. And, when you do make it at home, please, pretty please with a cherry on top, never ever slice it neatly into discs! Grate it. And don't bottle it. Not even for posterity. Thank you.

MR DREAM MAKER

There was a man in our neighbourhood in Grahamstown who wasn't even particularly hot, but whose nickname was Mr Dream Maker. Women kinda liked him, I guess. Mr Dream Maker walked around with swag, as if he were the gold stand-ard of manhood, of sex appeal and all things cool. I'm tempted to add to my memory of him, imagining him perhaps chewing apricot-flavoured Beechies. I always remember Mom greeting him heartily whenever he walked past our house in Albany Road, 'Mr Dream Maker! Hoezit!' She'd smile, he'd share a pleasantry, and swag on by.

The nickname was a reference to a hit by Judy Boucher. And it was a song you would find playing at many houses in the area every weekend, especially early on a Saturday morning. You would hear the bittersweet plea: 'How could my dreams be so mean to me?/When Heaven knows, I love you so/So please come back tomorrow night/Mr Dream Maker please turn my dreams around!'

Just thinking about Judy Boucher bring backs a flood of tear-filled memories. Not tears on my part but people, especially women, suffering *dronk verdriet* after drinking too much Esprit! It was almost as if they chose to depress themselves by listening to Judy Boucher's melancholic, addictive ballads on repeat, and volume turned up to the max! All of us, even as little kids, knew the lyrics of every single Judy Boucher track. We didn't fully understand those lyrics like the drunk adults who could not get enough of them, but we sang along while noticing that auntie so-and-so was looking teary-eyed while pouring herself another glass of beer from the quart of Lion Lager or, if she was more ladylike, sticking to Esprit.

There was so much heartbreak in my community. I guess that's why Judy Boucher was such a hit. And it wasn't all about women yearning for Mr Dream Maker. Actually, one of her most popular songs was the polyandrous lament of a woman who wished she could be with two lovers at the same time, regrettably telling one of them, 'If I could be in two places at the same time/believe me/I would share my love with you'. But, unfortunately, she tells him, 'Tonight I will only share my love with (my main lover)'. I wonder if it ever occurred to auntie so-and-so that this song celebrates cheating. I guess, if you romanticise the song long enough, Esprit in hand, you can pretend it is the ultimate expression of the tragedy of desiring two people at once. It happens. Even if we're told to only be with one.

This track, come to think of it, is filled with such sadness in the melody that, if you don't think about the lyrics much, you still feel huge sympathy for this cheat who is overcome with the burden of loving more than one person. She is a victim of Mother Nature having endowed her with an Ubuntu-like capacity to spread her love. But society, of course, dictates that she can only be with one (at a time). Poor her.

So loved was Judy Boucher in my area that people assumed she was coloured. To this day you would shock many people in my township if you had to break the news to them that Judy Boucher is not a coloured auntie with a nice voice who comes from Uitenhage! Boucher, who is in fact Caribbean, was shocked to learn of her popularity in South Africa. My Aunt Agnes still doesn't know. I hope no one ever tells her.

The only thing more nostalgic than simply listening to a Judy Boucher cassette would be to listen to it while you finish your plate of beetroot-accompanied Sunday lunch.

THE STORY OF OUR BLACK TAXED LIVES

One of the most important radio discussions I have had was about a phenomenon some of us call 'black tax'. I had friends on the show who were black professionals. One had studied engineering at Wits, and the other economics at UCT. I myself had studied philosophy and legal theory. We chatted, like *tjommies* at a braai, and with listeners as voyeurs who then joined the conversation, about the many forms of black tax we have to pay.

There was a story from one of my friends about how he had to pay for renovations at his mom's house, and for nephews to go to school, and was still expected to bring pocket money and gifts when visiting. Another friend had to pay for his sister at university, while still giving his mom a soft loan to buy goods which she could, in turn, sell in the hope of becoming a real entrepreneur, and there was little left for my friend to save or invest after all of that. Listeners, too, called in with a mix of funny and sad stories, but stories that were just familiar in the first instance.

One listener said she was judged by her white colleagues who assumed she must be really bad at handling her money. There had been a death in her family, and she had to take the Greyhound from Joburg to the rural areas to attend the funeral. And her white colleagues, who knew that she was earning more or less the same as they did, were puzzled that she could not simply have flown home. How, after all, could anyone who works for an investment bank or a management consulting firm in Sandton, for example, not have access to emergency cash or credit to jump on a plane if someone at home had died? The reason, of course, was that this young black female professional had been paying a lot of 'black tax' which left her cash-strapped; she was sending remittances home every month, and now she had to pay for the funeral expenses of this relative. Her monthly expenses were gigantic compared with those of her colleagues because she had an entire extended family with expectations of her to help them out.

I met a brilliant young strategy consultant recently who had been, while she was a student still, on a full scholarship that not only gave her good pocket money, but which also nurtured her to become an entrepreneur one day. The basis of the scholarship programme, one of the most useful in our country, is that if we can successfully persuade a generation of brilliant young business minds to become captains of industries rather than cogs in the wheels of existing corporates, it will be good for the economy. We will improve our economic growth figures if more, new successful companies create economic value for us; and we will reduce unemployment if new companies are able to employ the millions of South Africans currently out of work.

I was drawn to the brilliance of this consultant, and she struck me, unlike myself, as being excellent with cash, a good planner and as having a knack for granular detail. So, I assumed she was probably, on the side of an event I was moderating, going to tell me about her investments, the first apartment she had bought, and so on. I was wrong. She was held back by black tax. She could not, in fact, risk foregoing her regular monthly salary and take the plunge and try out her business idea. She didn't mind the personal consequence of such risk taking, but she had an extended family dependent on her financially. Her middle-class confidence and an accent that suggested private schooling were deceptive; they were not the sum total of her life's journey, her personal story, and the burdens that had been imposed on her as the first graduate in her family.

I was even more shocked when she told me that although she was at one of the world's top management consulting firms, she had, for her first two years there, been in credit card debt. Not because she was imprudent – in one sense, of course, racking up credit card debt is almost, one might say, inherently imprudent, but that is a hasty description of what had happened in this case – but she traded a poor credit record for satisfying the cash needs of her mom and other relatives who expected her degree to translate into a bottomless pit of money. She could only buy her first car when she was promoted from business analyst to associate, even though her business analyst salary probably already meant she was one of the top one per cent or two per cent of income earners in the country. Only with promotion did she manage to clear her credit card debt. Yet, for many white students who graduate from UCT with a business science degree, getting a job in the financial heartland of Sandton can mean cash that is immediately yours, and you can start saving and building wealth, rather than delaying wealth creation until you have paid black tax. Insignificant statistical exceptions aside, black tax is real; white tax isn't a thing. Don't tell me about that one white *oke* who's also poor.

And that was why that radio discussion was such an easy one to facilitate, and such a hit: tens of thousands of black professionals know the drill. We know the ways in which, especially if you're a first-generation university graduate, you are squeezed for cash by dependants. You can even, out of the blue, get a call from a cousin you have not spoken to in ten years who casually apologises for bothering you, insincerely tells you not to worry if you can't help them, but then asks you if you can't lend them R5 000 which they promise to pay back over three months from the end of next month. Of course they do not have the capacity to pay the money back, and they know that you may save yourself awkwardness by not demanding the money back. And so they rely on your sense of guilt that you left home for greener pastures, and hope the guilt translates into you depositing money into their accounts or maybe sending a smaller amount, right now, via cell phone banking.

Black tax is not simple, imprudent behaviour. It is about accepting that the one in the family who now has a salary has to make that salary stretch. And so just when you are tucking into a nice juicy steak with your other black professional friends, you might hold back on the dessert if you hear 'beep! beep!' and it is an SMS from a relative who wants money to buy Sunday lunch. Then you must choose between your dessert and paying for that Sunday's seven-colours lunch back home. It is your awkward reward for the privilege of escaping misery.

A friend who doesn't flaunt his access to credit drives a little Citi Golf that looks like it was bought from one of the rich schools that used it for driving lessons for rich kids doing the 'Driving Programme' in their matric year, but needed to be sold after it clocked over 100 000 kilometres already. But he doesn't care. He lives in Sandton, provides for his family and allows himself at least the indulgence of travelling as a just reward for working hard.

You could have hours of free flowing talk radio conversation knitting together these kinds of stories. It was almost a case of, as soon as one black professional was willing to confess to the pressures, everyone else felt they had the space to breathe. Beetroot and Judy Boucher might be good bittersweet nostalgia, but black tax is, *eish*, not so nice. But it is our reality and we get on with it. It is, actually, not so much tax as it is part of black culture – just like beet and Judy Boucher.

THE MISAPPROPRIATION OF BLACK MEMORY

When I first told the story of Judy Boucher, my black friends laughed out loud – well, virtually – on my Facebook wall with instant recognition. Some of my friends and I shared some memories in Afrikaans, in our Afrikaans, because the nostalgia wouldn't be as real in English if you grew up in an Afrikaans-speaking coloured neighbourhood. We experienced and lived *dronk verdriet* and Judy Boucher in Afrikaans.

Enter one of the nicest people in the world I met at Oxford: a really cool guy who is now an academic in England, brilliantly self-aware and 'conscious' and all that good stuff present in the heads and hearts of my favourite white South Africans, and he is like, 'Eusebius, actually Judy Boucher isn't just a black thing! I remember Judy Boucher ...' and off he rattles his own childhood memories of Boucher in his home. Park that thought.

More recently, when I posted a meme about black tax on my Facebook wall, another really sharp, awesome white American diplomat, now retired, made me feel bad when he posted something to the effect of, 'Eusebius, it happens in all families … I am a dad. My kid asks for money!' When I asked him to please allow us the particularities that come with black life and promised him – sarcastically to be fair on him – that we could transcend race the next day, he sheepishly got the point. But being a good debater who gives as much as he can take, he told me to flag the next time I am trying to start a discussion that is 'particular' to a group. I rejected the mild rebuke, and simply said he would not be warned next time but should rather work by himself, without my flagging anything, on the issue of when it is appropriate to hold back a wee bit before hitting the 'send' button, and simply listen and watch closely as a particular group's members exhibit aspects of their life alien to you. We left it there and, sure, I felt bad, again, as I do when well-meaning liberals seek commonalities with black people.

The same with beetroot. Some white people think it is the low point of race obsession to imagine that a widely eaten root – beet, for goodness sake! – could possibly have culturally specific resonance. Everyone eats it, after all, just as we all drink water, right? So why talk about black life and beetroot, they wonder.

This brings me, precisely, to what is innocent but misplaced here about my white friends wanting to rush to share their Judy Boucher memories or make a case for why black tax is actually a universal phenomenon or how they hated beetroot salad, too, as kids.

THE TORTUROUS YEARNING FOR UNIVERSALITY

There is an intense desire by some black people and many more white people in our country for race to be 'so last year!' These people want us to boldly go where no one has gone before. No, not just to infinity and beyond, but more ambitiously still to a land where racism's reach is no more, and the structures of racism are dismantled, and we are all just human beings with universal human traits, and thus we have all, in that imagined new world, 'transcended' race and the history of racism. I share that goal. But I do not pretend that our current reality is that place. To think that is to choose denial.

The structures of racism, such as institutionalised racism in educational spaces, not to mention racism that rears its head in interpersonal relationships between us, are too pervasive still for such transcendence to make sense. And that is why such projects aimed at searching for universal truths between groups, and suppressing particular experiences, should be called ex-actly what they are: avoidance – of the awkward and painful reality of racism's continuing presence and, more to the point when it comes to my white friends loving Judy Boucher and 'knowing' black tax, a simultaneous attempt to avoid *difference*.

Because, if you think about it, the flip side of thinking we have transcended race and racism is to assert that, *Simunye*, we are one! I have found that very often the advocates of race transcendence are also the ones who want to say that we all – black and white, poor and rich – have the same relationship with beetroot salad, Judy Boucher and 'family' tax. These advocates of commonalities think of these commonalities as glue that binds us together more strongly than our past divisions. It would be harsh to brand this kind of search for commonality as overtly racist.

But the search for universal truths is a consequence of racism's hold over us: a refusal to accept differences, as if doing so *constitutes* racism. That is why to acknowledge differences based on racial identities can be painful, because doing so is in part a concession that racism left a legacy that is still here. And because that legacy is odious, it is tempting to wish away *particular* group experiences and imagine us to have only *universal* cultural tropes rather than any tropes specific to particular groups.

The white friends I have referred to are certainly not racists, and I know this on the basis of familiarity with a larger slice of each of their life narratives than a reader of this essay has access to. So not every attempt to search for commonalities between us can be attributed to a racist motive. That would be absurd. But racism isn't absent in the explanation of this search for commonality. It is the attempt to avoid racism's legacy, to overcome it, that motivates a perpetual search for, and celebration of, commonality.

This is not to say only black people eat beetroot salad, or only coloured aunties have *dronk verdriet* while singing along to Judy Boucher and drinking Esprit, or that only black professionals have multiple claims on their monthly salary. But, as a friend and I chuckled when we chewed over the beetroot discussion, we can all eat beetroot salad but still have different cultural tropes that come with it. I honestly would be shocked to the core if even a big minority of white South Africans who regularly eat beetroot salad know the salad *as we know it*. Do you have long queues at a white funeral where the entire neighbourhood lines up for food to be dished out of huge pots that were prepared in anticipation of feeding over one hundred people – many who went neither to the church nor the graveside – and then topping up the plates of stew with beetroot served out of massive plastic basins? No? I thought so.

These particular tropes exist in South Africa precisely because of our racist past. Racist apartheid geography made sure that we lived apart. Living apart geographically was then compounded by linguistic, cultural, ethnic and class divisions. We never lived in each other's space. We still don't. So how could there possibly be an abundance of universal cultural experiences to foreground in a public narrative about a common national identity? It is all myth-making; it is an attempt to transcend racism rather than confronting and dismantling its remnants. And learning to live with differences that aren't inherently divisive.

So anyone who deems these particularities as exaggerated on my part are, frankly, implying that apartheid geography never happened and left no legacy. It happened. And its legacy is that a white dad sending his kids money isn't black tax. Beetroot from a Woolies jar doesn't appear at black funerals. Slices of beet on a white family's table isn't a send-off at a black funeral.

And Judy Boucher can be imagined to be from Uitenhage, but certainly not Sandton. Or so my auntie Agnes thinks.

WHAT ARE THE CONNECTIONS BETWEEN
RACISM'S LEGACY AND XENOPHOBIA?

HOW HAS RACISM AFFECTED
BLACK PEOPLE'S MORAL COMPASSES?

DO WHITE PEOPLE HAVE A MONOPOLY ON RACISM?

OUR DAMAGED
BLACK SELVES

THE KILLERS OF COUNTRY X

On the morning of 16 April 2015 I woke up around 4.30 am from a disturbing nightmare. I tried not to disturb my partner snoring next to me as I reached for my phone next to my side of the bed. There is a little passageway that leads to an *en suite* bathroom in our apartment and the door to it was ajar. I could see through the blinds of the bathroom window that it was pitch-dark outside. I tried to convince myself that, despite the darkness outside, it was already morning. I was hoping I would *not* be sleep-deprived despite the nightmare I had just had.

I had dreamt that I was a foreign visitor in a country somewhere on another planet, and I was with a female friend. My nameless friend and I had visited this country, country X, excited to be touring and checking out opportunities to maybe work or live there, or just to get to know the locals. When we got to the city centre, however, we found ourselves in a world that was far from the romantic depictions of the country in brochures which showcased its beauty and praised its diversity.

Our first barrier was language: no one spoke our tongue, and anyone we tried to interact with was mortally and violently offended that we were unable to speak the local language. All around us were dead bodies. I felt an anxiety attack coming on, and my nameless friend seemed like she was losing her sanity fast. We could both feel the fear of death and the noxious, nauseating smell of death itself. We were suddenly dumb, like zombies; too stunned to speak.

It quickly became apparent that the dead and the dying were also visitors in the land of X, so we hid behind buildings as we saw the killers marching around. We instantly knew that our own lives were in danger.

But the strangest thing was depicted in the next snapshot of the nightmare that refused to fade: nameless friend and I heard voices – people fluent in our own language. We ran towards them. There were about ten teenagers, all looking like tik addicts from the Cape Flats, speaking with the same accents, looking dishevelled and forgotten, and yet without the fear we were experiencing. It was puzzling. We struck up a conversation and they told us that they had grown up there, that their parents had moved to X to escape the worst of the land of their origins, our own South Africa. They had hoped to find a land of opportunity, but in fact they were simply struggling to survive because the locals had become hostile to their parents. I listened, still too scared to speak freely, glancing over my shoulders to see if the killers were in sight. Before saying goodbye, we asked about a taxi to the airport. Nameless friend and I had decided to end our visit to X and get out of the war zone.

The next few snapshots confronted my half-awake self like a pack of cards strewn on a table. As nameless friend and I walked down a street; several taxi signs could be seen on top of each car. The road was untarred and the vehicles themselves seemed like they were put together at a rubbish site. As I approached the first car, the driver disappeared into thin air and the taxi sign vanished. I convinced myself that my eyes had deceived me and that there had been no driver in the first car all along. We approached the next car and could see the driver sitting in the front seat. Nameless friend was clutching my hand as we jogged towards the car. Then I blinked. And each blink was a moment of relief, a respite from being a witness to war. But when my eyes could see again, after just one little blink, the driver in this second car had turned into a dog. We sprinted in the opposite direction.

Suddenly, we noticed the killers. They were coming for us. It made no sense. Why were the people of country X turning on us? Sure, we were aliens, but we came in peace! We ran into an empty house, straight through the front door. The place reeked of conflict, attack, escape. We ran straight out the back door and jumped the fence into another yard, feeling the approach of the killers of the land of X.

A small flat next door had people inside it talking in hushed tones. We knocked and entered without permission. Three men who seemed high on drugs stared at us. They were locals, but whatever they had smoked or ingested or sniffed seemed to have pacified them. Could we trust them? Was this a safe house? Or were all the people of country X killers? I was scared to know the answer, but we could not keep running. We *had* to take a chance and speak to The Three Strangers. But they too did not speak our language. After many weird sign-language attempts, they seemed to understand that we wanted a ride in the car parked outside. I made a gesture of flying, and assumed their affirming body language meant they knew we wanted to be taken to the airport. So we jumped in the car. Two of The Strangers were in the front, one in the driver's seat and the other in the front passenger seat. I was seated in the back, behind the front left passenger seat. The third of The Strangers sat next to me, and my nameless friend sat behind the driver.

Suddenly, the inside of the car seemed bigger than before and The Three Strangers were no longer high. The one next to me turned into a dog and started growling. The car was still moving and yet the driver had somehow managed to join us in the back. How he got there, I do not know. But I did know that, like the other foreigners we had seen in the city centre, we were about to die. The driver, laughing now, sat on the floor space between the driver's seat and the dangling feet of my nameless friend. He took her left foot, laughed with enormous pleasure, and started hacking it with the sharp edge of a blade attached to an axe-like weapon he was wielding. He chopped the soles of both feet like Mom chopped onions in the kitchen when I was a kid. There was one difference: Mom cried; this killer was laughing.

It was at this point that I arose from my bed, rushed to my bathroom and took a hot shower, although a cold one might have been more therapeutic. Then I boiled the kettle to make a cup of bitter, black coffee as the birds, mercifully, started chirping. The shaft of early-morning light through the blinds in my kitchen soothed me. I tried to shut the forensic report of my nightmare in my head, but could not help myself speculating about it. I realised that what I encountered on social media just before I fell asleep the night before had set me up for a nightmare.

THE DEATH OF OUR HUMANITY

At the time of my nightmare in 2015 our country was seeing some of the worst xenophobic attacks on foreign nationals living in South Africa. The scenes in my nightmare, especially of one of the bodies in the city centre, were identical to the images making the rounds on social media depicting what we, as South Africans, were doing to foreigners in Durban, Johannesburg and elsewhere. Whether some of the pictures were dated or new is a discussion I have avoided. Because, frankly, whether a foreign national was killed in 2008 or in 2015 doesn't change the fact that we killed him because he was not 'one of us'. Dating the picture of his burning body won't bring him back to life.

We were violently brutal towards fellow Africans and other foreign nationals. The critical question to explore is what the genesis of this black-on-black racism is. Denying its reality is irresponsible.

One of those pictures on social media showed a man in flames, crying in anguish, with two police officers in the background running in his direction. If you thought the police were there to keep the peace, to rescue the man, or try battle the furnace that was previously his body, you are wrong. One of the two police officers wears a smirk on his face as if bemused. This particular photo may well be one of the dated ones, but the date's irrelevance was brought home to me in one of the last reports I read on my phone before falling asleep.

In Durban, where an assault on humanity had started a few days earlier, a reporter interviewed some of the victims. One of them said that they did not trust our police. They made the chilling observation that some of the police held back on their own violent xenophobic instincts while wearing police uniform but joined the mobs when they were not. And this fellow African brother could not trust that the police uniform guaranteed that the same man who could kill in civilian clothing was a friend when in uniform. That remark seemed to be confirmed in the image of the police officer seemingly delighting in being a perverse witness to a xenophobic attack.

For some reason, it was not the photos of the dead that disturbed me most. It was the photos, and even mere descriptions on social media, of the survivors that would not leave me. Death is the ultimate obliteration of a person – I know that, of course. But, tragically, non-existence can also be relief from sustained pain and violence. One person had a Facebook update about a camp they had visited that temporarily sheltered victims of xenophobia. One of the victims had been attacked with a screwdriver on the side of his face. It had pierced his flesh and bone and injured his eye. The assault on his dignity didn't end there: a hospital refused to treat him, saying that it had a limit on the number of foreigners it was prepared to treat. Even the Hippocratic Oath was abandoned in a time of xenophobic evil. This survivor's pain continued, not disrupted by the finality of death.

One photo showed a victim whose back was hacked about five times, like a watermelon divided into parts with the help of a panga. We did not see the man's face in this photo. We just saw the back with the gashes in different places. I think, but can't be sure, that the reason this picture in particular stayed with me was because the man was alive. There was almost something nonchalant or banal even about his being alive, as if what had happened to him was just a fact of foreigner life in South Africa, and tomorrow the struggle to live would continue. This refusal to die, or to return to war-ridden countries of origin, isn't just gallant, it also means that, unlike corpses that can be taken away, this survivor's existence will be a living monument to our xenophobic evil. It is harder to deny my own evil when I see my victim getting on with it. It is easier to lack a conscience about my evil when my victim is buried, and is now out of sight.

RACISM'S LAST LAUGH

We are violent because of a combination of factors: living in the shadows of a police state (which was one of the inherent features of the apartheid state); violent notions of masculinity that South African men, myself included, have internalised and act out daily; deep inequality that breeds resentment, self-hate and a toxic sense of despair among the worst-off; state-sponsored violence that makes us use violence with each other, domestically; state-sponsored violence during peaceful, democratic times like the Marikana massacre and police brutality showing the rupture from the apartheid state has not been completed fully; and so on.

The trickier question is one we avoid like the plague because it is genuinely hard to answer: how do we unlearn violence? How do we habituate ourselves to live differently? Or are we doomed to be perpetually violent until the second coming of the Lord? How do we recover parts of our humanity that we lost in the war against colonialism and apartheid, a struggle that is ongoing and making work on the damaged black self difficult to prioritise?

Often, of course, 'humanity' is a word, a term, that can be rather wistfully thrown around to skewer someone morally if they lack 'humanity', or to lavish someone with praise for showing it off in abundance. It is important to be clear what one means by this important word. By 'humanity' I am trying to capture, in part, an ability to feel *for others* and project yourself into their body. In addition, humanity is about having due regard for the interests of others in your reasoning about how to act in the world. Humanity, in this sense, does not require sophisticated education or even a complex linguistic skill set. We have an innate capacity for empathy, but different life narratives may affect the likelihood of any particular person's moral compass functioning.

Colonialism and apartheid have tragically damaged the moral compasses of many black South Africans. This is why we show a reduced humanity towards fellow Africans. We have learned to hate, like Verwoerd hated us, and we have learned how not to project ourselves into the bodies of people who are different from ourselves. We have learned not to give due regard to the interests of foreign nationals, an entitlement that flows simply from them being human. Instead, when we do reason morally (if at all), we uncritically rank people from the region into categories of different levels of entitlement to respect, just like the apartheid government ranked us with legislated arbitrary criteria. This is itself a legacy of racism. Racism, sadly, runs in our blood. White people do not have a monopoly on racism. Xenophobia and Afrophobia (a fear of, deep disdain for, and even hatred towards, fellow Africans) are intimately connected to the legacies of colonialism and racism.

And it's not just our democratic state showing these deep stains of racism with our initial refusal to call xenophobia exactly what it is: xenophobia. The same applies to us citizens. It is troubling how many fellow South Africans have tried to walk the fine line, unsuccessfully, between 'making sense' of xenophobia and *excusing* it. Poverty is not a justification for hating foreign nationals. And economic injustice, as a result of your own government and fellow South Africans not sharing the spoils of freedom with you, does not give you justified reason to kill foreign nationals. Not even a politically and morally incendiary speech by a monarch – call him, for the sake of argument, King Goodwill Zwelithini – justifies lashing out against people who look different from us.

And yet a number of middle-class, self-styled allies of the poor have engaged in moral relativism sold to critics as a search for complexity and understanding. There is nothing complex about compromising your own humanity and that of another person in an act of racist, xenophobic violence. But these class allies of the poor, some of them leaders or members of civil society organisations founded on the promotion of social justice and human rights, tell us not to be too outraged. We are scolded, the rest of us, for expressing moral outrage on social media platforms, the implication being that critics of xenophobia would get the anger and frustration of the perpetrators of this violence if we lived with them or at least engaged them on why they were turning on foreign nationals.

But this is nonsense. It is intellectual pussyfooting. Always be wary of the person who tells you, 'It's more complicated than you think!' Sometimes that will be true, but too often it is a claim that is designed to deny an uncomfortable reading of plain truth. In this case, there is no moral complexity. Just a plain, uncomfortable truth that the illegal and immoral attacks on foreign nationals cannot be justified.

This precarious straddling of the explanation–justification divide is actually all about making middle-class people feel better about themselves. If middle-class South Africans really cared for the indigent we would see more cross-class solidarity on a daily basis and during peaceful times when violence doesn't flare up. How many of these allies of the xenophobes think long and hard about their personal responsibility to help reduce the inequities and poverty in society that ripen the atmosphere for xenophobia? Very few of us, if we are honest. This means that the attempt to 'understand' why poor South Africans are doing this to foreigners living among us is an attempt, on the part of allies of the poor, to evade personal responsibility for gross and unjust levels of inequality in our country that set up conditions conducive to violence.

If you can rationalise why the worst-off in your society are behaving like the animals from my nightmare, and your explanation leaves your own agency out of the picture, then you can switch off the news for a little while and enjoy your glass of wine on your balcony in the suburbs feeling you are above the fray. Ultimately, this attempt to 'complicate' xenophobia is itself xenophobic: we, as middle-class South Africans, are so anti-foreigner ourselves that we become allies of the most violent xenophobes in our midst. We prioritise an *explanation* of violence over the immediate and more urgent expression of unequivocal moral disapproval of the violence. Just because we've done little or nothing to help poor South Africans live more flourishing lives does not mean we should prop up xenophobes. Poverty is an injustice. But that doesn't mean the poor are immune to criticism for acts of *in*justice. And explanations of xenophobia that in effect render victims of xenophobia as dispensable in the expression of poor people's outrage, themselves count as evidence that many of us wealthier South Africans are as xenophobic as many poor South Africans. We just use wayward moral reasoning that doesn't leave a corpse in the road or a gash on a back. But we are no different from poor black South Africans.

CONCLUDING THOUGHT: RACISM'S REACH

Xenophobia is not disconnected from racism. One of the most unspoken-about consequences of anti-black racism is that we ourselves as black people have memory of how to be racist and we are capable of mimicking colonisers. This means that even if white people disappeared in a puff of magic, and all statues of colonialists were toppled, we would still not be free of the consequences of racism's history, a history we cannot undo. That is a profoundly disturbing reality that many fellow black South Africans do not want to own up to. But, I'm afraid, victims of racism, like victims of sexual abuse, can become the next generation of racists, and the next generation of sexual predators. The bad news for the state, for middle-class South Africans, and for the poor is that, not only are we xenophobic, but we also seem to have become clones of the racists who taught us how to hate on the basis of arbitrary differences between us.

In the end, however, we can't be let off the hook morally. My nightmare of killers in country X turning into dogs might be disturbing imagery, but it is only a nightmare. Dogs act from instinct. They are beasts. They cannot be held legally or morally accountable. They do not have the ability to step back from their actions, contemplate, and reason morally, let alone be influenced by their non-existent capacity for moral reasoning.

We are not dogs. We are not beasts. We are not robots. We remain persons, even with the deep scars of racism's past all around us and in us. That means we have the capacity to behave differently from how we behaved yesterday. It is entirely up to each one of us whether or not we confront and eliminate our ingrained racism handed down from colonial and apartheid architects and foot soldiers. And it is up to as a community to call each other out.

A question that haunts me is this: will racism's architects always have the last laugh?

CPSIA information can be obtained at www.ICGtesting.com
Printed in the USA
LVOW08s0733221215

467460LV00003B/7/P